P9-DDD-196

THE ENERGY BUS

10 Rules
to Fuel Your Life, Work, and Team
with Positive Energy

JON GORDON

John Wiley & Sons, Inc.

Copyright © 2007 by Jon Gordon. All rights reserved.

Published by John Wiley & Sons, Inc., Hoboken, New Jersey.
Published simultaneously in Canada.

No part of this publication may be reproduced, stored in a retrieval system, or
transmitted in any form or by any means, electronic, mechanical, photocopying,
recording, scanning, or otherwise, except as permitted under Section 107 or 108 of
the 1976 United States Copyright Act, without either the prior written permission of
the Publisher, or authorization through payment of the appropriate per-copy fee to
the Copyright Clearance Center, Inc., 222 Rosewood Drive, Danvers, MA 01923,
(978) 750-8400, fax (978) 646-8600, or on the web at www.copyright.com. Requests
to the Publisher for permission should be addressed to the Permissions Department,
John Wiley & Sons, Inc., 111 River Street, Hoboken, NJ 07030, (201) 748-6011,
fax (201) 748-6008, or online at http://www.wiley.com/go/permissions.

Limit of Liability/Disclaimer of Warranty: While the publisher and author have used
their best efforts in preparing this book, they make no representations or warranties
with respect to the accuracy or completeness of the contents of this book and
specifically disclaim any implied warranties of merchantability or fitness for a
particular purpose. No warranty may be created or extended by sales
representatives or written sales materials. The advice and strategies contained
herein may not be suitable for your situation. You should consult with a
professional where appropriate. Neither the publisher nor author shall be liable for
any loss of profit or any other commercial damages, including but not limited to
special, incidental, consequential, or other damages.

For general information on our other products and services or for technical support,
please contact our Customer Care Department within the United States at
(800) 762-2974, outside the United States at (317) 572-3993 or fax (317) 572-4002.

Wiley also publishes its books in a variety of electronic formats. Some content that
appears in print may not be available in electronic books. For more information
about Wiley products, visit our web site at www.wiley.com.

Library of Congress Cataloging-in-Publication Data:

Gordon, Jon, 1971–
    The energy bus : 10 rules to fuel your life, work, and team with positive
energy / Jon Gordon.
        p.   cm.
    ISBN-13: 978-0-470-10028-8 (cloth)
    1. Teams in the workplace—Management.   2. Employee motivation.   3.
Motivation (Psychology)   I. Title.
    HD66.G665   2007
    650.1—dc22   2006024223

Printed in the United States of America.

50   49   48   47   46

To my mother, Nancy Gordon Nicolosi

*Your strength and courage in the face of cancer will
always inspire me. I love you from the depths of my heart.*

Contents

Foreword

In many of my seminars I begin by asking people to stand up and do two things. First, I ask them to greet other people as if they are unimportant. After an initial chuckle or two, there's a dull hum as everyone walks around trying to ignore each other. Then I stop them and ask them to continue to greet people, but this time, to do it as if the people they are greeting are long-lost friends they're glad to see. The room erupts with laughter and the volume rises as people run around, smiling, hugging, and chatting with each other.

When the people in the audience sit down, I ask them, "Why do you think I had you do those two things—besides the fact that I'm from California?"

After the audience laughs, I tell them that the answer is positive energy. "To run a successful organization," I say, "you must learn to manage people's energy, including your own. When was there more energy in the room—during the first activity or the second?"

Of course, everyone shouts out, "The second!"

"What did I do to change the energy in the room?" I ask. Then I answer: "All I did was change your focus from a negative thought to a positive thought, and the energy of the room increased tenfold."

What I just described to you is why I'm excited about Jon Gordon and *The Energy Bus*. Every morning you have a choice. Are you going to be a positive thinker or a negative thinker? Positive thinking will energize you.

When you get to work, you have another choice. You can catch people doing things right, or you can catch them doing things wrong. Guess which of those two activities energizes people more?

If you want to fuel your family, your career, your team, and your organization with spirit, read this book. Jon's energy and advice will leap off the page and help you cultivate positive energy in everything you do—and you will make the world a better place for your having been here.

Thanks, Jon, for pumping us up and making sure we get on the right bus.

—Ken Blanchard
Co-author of *The One Minute Manager*®
and *Leading at a Higher Level*

Acknowledgments

I truly believe that no one ever creates success alone. Everyone needs a positive team with supportive people at their side. I am thankful that I have been blessed with truly amazing people on my bus and journey through life.

First I must thank the driver of my family's bus, my wife, Kathryn. You are the glue that keeps us together. Your support has made all the difference. Without you I would not be the man I am today. And I thank my children, Jade and Cole, for reminding me what matters most. Every day you make me want to be a better father. My favorite part of the day is asking about your success at bedtime. I love you.

My parents get a big thank you for always cheering as my bus drove on. You were invariably there supporting and loving me every step of the way.

Thank you to my brother for always challenging me and helping me improve this book. Your ideas, suggestions, and encouragement helped make this book the best it could be. I look forward to seeing your book next to mine in the bookstore. Also, special thanks to my grandfather Eddy, who at the age of 89 inspires me to live young, have fun, and enjoy the ride.

Thank you to my Chief Energy Officer, Daniel Decker. You are not just a business partner, but a true friend who has helped me grow as a leader and as a person. I appreciate every ounce of energy you pour into our mission. I am thankful God brought us together on the same bus.

Thank you to my friends and agents, Arielle Ford and Brian Hilliard. You have helped me pave the way to do the work I am here to do and I am forever grateful. You helped open the gates so my bus could drive through. Thank you for your confidence in me.

Thank you to Kate Lindsay, Shannon Vargo, Matt Holt, and the incredible team at John Wiley & Sons for seeing my vision for the road ahead and for making it possible.

To the other members of my team who not only provided fuel for our bus ride but who also got out and helped push when the bus broke down: Francis Ablola, thank you for all your hard work and web site creation. Shawn O'Shell, thank you for your amazing talent and design. Vince Bagni and Jim Careccia, thank you for continuing to spread the energy. Susan, thanks for the gifts you share with others.

Thank you to all my clients who allow me to work with your companies, organizations, teams, and people. I am grateful every day to get to work with so many wonderful people.

I'd like to thank Ken Blanchard, Danny Gans, Pat Williams, Dwight Cooper, Fran Charles, Linda Sherrer,

Tom Gegax, Mac Anderson, and all the people who read and supported the book.

I'd like to thank all the subscribers to my weekly newsletter and the readers of my books. You have shared your life stories, your hearts, your pain, and your triumphs with me and I am honored that you trust me to be a part of your life and growth. We are all teachers and students and I learn so much from you.

Most of all I'd like to thank God. Thank you for the signs that show me the way. Thank you for the gift of Jesus. Your holy spirit flowed through me as I wrote this book. You strengthen me and you are the ultimate driver of my Energy Bus.

xi

Acknowledgments

Author's Note

It is fun to look back at your life and see how certain events led to where you are right now, like the inspiration to write this book. I was traveling on a 28-city book tour for my first book, *Energy Addict: 101 Ways to Energize Your Life*, when I met an actual bus driver who took me from the Denver rental car lot to the airport. The bus driver not only had the biggest smile I had ever seen but dispensed life-changing wisdom that truly impacted me. This bus driver embodied the positive energy I was traveling the country talking about. I wrote an article about this meeting in my weekly e-newsletter called "10 Rules for the Ride of Your Life" and was inundated with enthusiastic responses calling it the best newsletter yet. Then one day while taking a walk the idea and story for this book just literally jumped into my head. And once I started writing, I couldn't stop. The words flowed through me, and now you are holding this book.

So it is my pleasure to invite you on the Energy Bus

as we take a short, fun, meaningful journey together. I hope you use this book not only to fuel your life, work, and team with positive energy but also to enjoy the ride of your life. After all, the goal in life is to live young, have fun, and arrive at your final destination—as late as possible—with a smile on your face, because this would mean that you truly enjoyed the ride.

I'd like to also give credit to the following people and work for inspiring certain ideas in this book.

Words from the Energy Bus children's book were inspired by Richard Bach, the author of *Illusions* and *Jonathan Livingston Seagull*, who said, "You are never given a wish without the power to make it come true."

The positive energy formula was inspired by the formula E + R = 0, which Jack Canfield, author of *The Success Principles*, shared with me.

The information from the Energy Book referred to in the story is from my book *The 10-Minute Energy Solution*.

The story about Abraham Lincoln waiting for Civil War battle reports to come in was inspired by an audio recording from Jim Collins, author of *Good to Great*. But while Jim Collins also talks about getting the right people on the bus, the idea for this book was my own.

I learned about the airplane design study for rule #9 from Laurie Beth Jones and her book, *Jesus CEO*.

Research about the energy of the heart was from the

Institute of HeartMath, www.heartmath.org. They are doing phenomenal and innovative work.

Joy's bus was number 11 for a reason. It's a special number to me.

I'm sending positive energy your way,

Jon

Introduction

Positive energy. . . . It's a term being talked about a lot more frequently in conference rooms, classrooms, locker rooms, and even living rooms. Perhaps it's because there is an abundance of new research that shows that positive people, positive communication, positive interactions, and positive work and team cultures produce positive results. Or perhaps at a deeper level we all know that every person, every career, every company, every organization, every family, and every team will have to overcome negativity, adversity, and challenges to define themselves and create success.

No one goes through life untested, and the answer to these tests is positive energy—not the rah-rah, cheering kind of positive energy, although there certainly is a time and a place for that as well. But rather, when I talk about positive energy I'm referring to the optimism, trust, enthusiasm, love, purpose, joy, passion, and spirit to live, work, and perform at a higher level; to build and lead successful teams; to overcome adversity in life and at work; to share contagious energy with employees, colleagues, and customers; to bring out the best in others and in yourself; and to overcome all the negative people (whom I call energy vampires) and negative situations that threaten to sabotage your health, family, team, and success.

Positive energy is very real, and in my work with thousands of leaders, salespeople, teams, coaches, organizations, teachers, athletes, moms, dads, and even children, I have witnessed the amazing power of positive energy. I have seen principals turn their schools around and enhance morale. Leaders have told me how they used my strategies to help their employees and teams become more successful. Cancer survivors have told me how they won with a positive attitude. Athletes have shared how they've overcome adversity to reach their goal. Hardworking employees have e-mailed me and told me countless stories of promotions and accomplishments at work. And one mom even called to tell me a story about her son Joshua who, after hearing that his mom and dad were getting a divorce, said he was going to try to be strong and positive through it all because positive people live longer, happier, and healthier lives. It turns out Joshua remembered what I said to him a year earlier when I spoke at his school about the importance of positive energy. Not only was I touched, but I was deeply inspired.

People like Joshua inspire me to write about and share positive energy because deep down I know it matters and I know it works. My hope is that you will use this book to cultivate positive energy in your own life and career and then share it with your colleagues, customers, organization, team, friends, and family. I'm confident that when you apply the principles in this book you'll find greater happiness, enhanced success, higher performance, inspired teamwork, and significant results.

While this fable takes place in a business setting, please know that this book was written for everyone. We all are part of a team, and every member of our team—whether it's our work team, sports team, family team, church team, or school team—can benefit from the 10 simple, powerful rules shared in this book. After all, positive people and positive teams produce positive results, and the essential ingredient is positive energy.

Chapter 1

Flat Tire

 It was Monday and Mondays were never good for George. He stood in his driveway looking at his car and shaking his head. He wasn't surprised, really. Misfortune had been following him for the past few years like a dark rain cloud hovering over his life, and today was no different. His tire was completely flat, and George's face was about to burst. "Not today!" he shouted as he opened the trunk only to find a flat spare tire.

He heard his wife's words in his head: "You should get that fixed, George. One day you're going to have a flat and wish you had a spare tire."

Why does she always have to be right? he wondered. George thought of his neighbor Dave and ran down the block to see if he had already left for work. Dave worked downtown, too, and George was hoping to catch a quick ride with him.

George had an important meeting with his team at work, and today he couldn't afford to be late. Not today. Especially not today. George punched the air with his

1

clenched fist when he saw that Dave's car was gone. Of course, he thought. Why would he still be here? That would be too easy.

As sweat poured from his brow, he ran back home, then stood in his driveway and looked at his cell phone trying to think of someone at work he could call. Think, think think, think think.

Then it dawned on him. He couldn't think of one person at work he could call who would come pick him up. His only option left was his wife, and she was the last person he wanted to ask.

George walked in the house and heard the usual noise and chaos coming from the kitchen. He could hear the puppy jumping around and his wife trying to get the kids to sit still and eat their breakfast before heading off to school. He peered through the kitchen archway. As soon as the children saw him, the cheers erupted. "Hi, Daddy!" they yelled. His daughter came up to him and wrapped her arms around his hip. "I love you, Daddy," she said as George barely acknowledged her. His son shouted, "Dad, can we play basketball right now?" George was like a reluctant celebrity in his own home. They wanted a piece of him, but he just wanted to hide in silence.

"No!" George shouted back. "It's not a weekend. I have to get to work. Now both of you just please be quiet so I can ask your mother something. Honey, I have a flat tire and I have this really important meeting I have to get to today and I need your car!" he said frantically.

"What about the spare?" she asked.

"Of course you would bring that up. I never got it fixed."

"Well, I can't help you, George. I have to take the kids to school, then I have a dentist appointment, then I have to get the puppy to the vet, then I have a parent-teacher meeting. Should I continue? You're not the only one who has things to do. You act like you're the only important one in this family, but I run this house and this family and if I don't have a car today, I can't do *my* job." She had become good at mounting a good offense to preempt George's attacks.

"Yes, but if I'm late to this meeting, then I may not have a job," he said.

As George and his wife continued bantering back and forth, their five-month-old puppy decided to say hello to George as well by jumping and slobbering all over him until he grabbed her by the collar and took her into her kennel. "Why did we get that dog, anyway?" he asked. "Do we really need to deal with a dog right now with all we have going on?"

"That's real nice," his wife said as their daughter started to cry, saying, "Daddy doesn't love Sammy."

"I can't deal with this right now," George said.

"You can't seem to deal with anything anytime," his wife countered.

"Can you just drop me off after taking the kids to school?" he asked. "I'll still probably make it in time for the meeting."

3

Flat Tire

"I don't have time, George. Didn't you hear all I have to do today? I'll hit serious traffic on the way back and then my day is gone. Why don't you just take the bus?" she said. "It's only about a mile to the bus stop."

"The bus? Are you kidding me? The bus! I haven't ridden on a bus since who knows when. Who takes the bus?" George asked, very frustrated.

"Well, today," his wife answered bluntly, "you do. That's who."

"Fine," George said as he grabbed his bag, stormed out of the house, and began his mile-long trek to the bus stop.

Bus #11 stopped in front of George, who was huffing, puffing, and swearing under his breath. What a surprise, George thought. I actually made the bus. With my luck I figured I would miss it.

As George stepped on the bus, he made eye contact with the driver, who had the two brightest eyes and the biggest smile he had ever seen.

"Good day to you today, Sugar!" she cheered.

George just grumbled and took his seat. What's so good about it? he thought.

But her eyes never left him as she watched him walk to his seat through her rearview mirror.

George could feel her eyes on him. Why is she looking at me? I paid the fare, he thought.

He could see her big, never-ending smile in the rearview mirror and wondered, Does this woman ever stop smiling? Doesn't she know it's Monday? Who smiles on Monday?

4

"Where you going?" she asked.

George pointed to himself. "Me?"

"Yeah, you, Sugar. I haven't seen you on my bus before and I know everyone on this route."

"To work at the NRG Company," he answered.

"That building downtown with the big lightbulb on it?" she asked excitedly.

"Yes, we make lightbulbs," answered George, who wished he had had time to get a paper so he could bury his head in it.

"So what do we owe the pleasure of having you on my bus today?" she asked.

"Flat tire," he said. "I hate taking the bus but I have a meeting I have to get to with my team and I had no other choice."

"Well, you just sit back, relax, and don't worry about a thing. You may not like taking the bus but I gotta tell you this is no ordinary bus. This is *my* bus and you're going to enjoy the ride. My name is Joy. What's yours?"

George mumbled his name hoping she would just leave him alone. His words were short and so was his fuse. Even on his best days George was not a man who enjoyed chitchatting, and he certainly didn't feel like talking to a bus driver who seemed like she had drunk one too many cups of coffee and of all names hers had to be Joy. Figures, he thought. Joy was something that had certainly been lacking in his life. He couldn't remember the last time he was happy. I bet she has no worries, he thought. All she has to do is drive a bus each day and smile and be nice to strangers. Sure, she can be all cheery and smile at me, but she knows nothing about me. She doesn't know the stress I deal with each day. She doesn't know the responsibilities I face at work and at home. Wife, boss, kids, employees, deadlines, mortgage, car payment, and a mom who is sick with cancer. She doesn't know how drained I feel.

But she *did know*. Every day they walked on and off her bus, and she could spot them immediately. They came in all shapes, ages, colors, and sizes: men, women, white, black, Asian, white collar, and blue collar. Yet all had a similar energy about them. She could see and feel it immediately. Lifeless. No kick in their step. Like a light had been turned off inside them. She could tell the people who shone brightly and those who had a subtle dim. She called them Dimmers. They walked around like zombies just trying to get through the day. No purpose, no spirit. No energy. As if it had been sucked out of them by the daily grind of life. She could tell the men who had given up their dreams. She knew the women who were working by day and taking care of a family by night. And she heard the complaints all the time. Too many people were overstressed, overtired, and overworked. That's why she made it her mission to be an Energy Ambassador and to try to energize everyone who came on her bus. That's why she called her ride the Energy Bus. And if anyone could use an energy boost, it was George.

"You know you came on my bus for a reason, George," she said firmly to him. "Everyone does."

George snapped back, "No, I came on your bus because I had a flat tire."

"You can choose to look at it that way, George, or you can see the big picture here. Everything happens for a reason. Don't forget that. Every person we meet. Every event in our life. Every flat tire happens for a reason. You can choose to ignore it or ask what that reason is and try to learn from it. Every problem has a gift for you in its hands as my man Richard Bach says. You can choose to see the curse or the gift. And this one choice will determine if your life is a success story or one big soap opera. And while I love soap operas, George, I don't like seeing real life people like you living them. And George, I got to tell you that from the look of you, you're not making the right choice. So choose wisely, George, *choose wisely.*"

At that the bus stopped and George got off as fast as he could, feeling more like he had been hit by a bus rather than riding on one. "Choose wisely; soap opera" stuck in his head. Whatever, he thought and shrugged it off. His team was waiting for him and he hated being late.

Joy didn't always like hitting her passengers straight between the eyes with the truth, but with the stubborn ones like George, she knew there was no other way. It was the stubborn ones who often had the most potential. She knew because many years ago she had been just like him. Down, out, tired, and negative. People had offered help but she had never accepted it. She had been angry at the world and hadn't thought she deserved it. It was ironic how the people who needed help the most were often the most closed off from receiving it. She had had a big coat of armor just like George did now, so sometimes the blunt truth was the only way through it. Joy figured she would never see George again but hoped that at least her piercing words would do some good.

Chapter 2

Good News and Bad News

That evening George sat in the car repair shop waiting for his tire to be replaced. It was taking much longer than it should and as usual George was growing anxious and impatient. He didn't like waiting: waiting in lines for the movies, waiting in traffic, or waiting in line at the grocery store. He always picked the wrong line and of course the person in front of him always had a product without a price tag so a manager needed to be called and the product had to be found and well, you know. George felt as if the world conspired to inconvenience him. How long could it take to replace a tire? he wondered.

At last the mechanic walked briskly into the room. "Sir, I've got some good news and some bad news. The good news is that your car isn't destroyed and you're still here."

"What are you talking about!" George shouted. "It's only a flat tire!"

"Well, that's more good news, Sir. The flat tire prevented you from driving the car. While replacing the tire,

I remembered seeing a notice from the manufacturer about your make and model so I had a hunch to do a check on the brakes and sure enough they were completely worn down. At any moment they could have gone, and you would have had no way of stopping. If you had hit a wall or something, you would be as flat as your tire. You're lucky to be here, Sir. It's been a common problem with your year, make, and model and you should have received notification of the recall."

George remembered seeing some letter from his car manufacturer but had just thought it was another sale mail trying to take his money and so he had thrown it away.

"The bad news," the mechanic continued, "is that the part takes about two weeks to get here from the manufacturer, so we'll need to keep the car here and once the part comes in we'll be able to have it ready that day."

Just great, George thought, not even realizing the good news he had just heard. The only things he was thinking about were having his car in the shop for two weeks and getting home. Just one more inconvenience for an inconvenient life.

Chapter 3

The Long Walk Home

 Instead of calling his wife to come get him, George decided to walk home the two or so miles from the repair shop. He walked more today than he had in several years, but at this point he didn't feel like talking to anyone, especially his wife. Car in the repair shop for two weeks, he thought. What else could go wrong? He was near his breaking point. Just last night his wife had told him she was unhappy in their marriage and that George's negativity was making the entire family miserable. She had given him an ultimatum. Change or it was over. It wasn't the first of their marital problems and certainly it wasn't the first time she had told George he was negative. But now it was real and he didn't want to lose the woman he loved. He knew she loved him, too, but, as she had said no matter how much she loved him, she wouldn't live with someone who made her life so miserable.

He vowed to change but for the first time in his life he was at a loss. He felt like his life was spinning out of control and he couldn't do anything to stop it. He had always been able to fix every problem and rise to every occasion to meet any challenge, especially in his marriage, yet now he felt truly powerless. As if his life was being lived by someone else while he watched it unravel. That night he had yelled to the heavens asking for help and had woken up with a flat tire. Some help, he thought. Just one more problem I don't need right now.

George walked briskly hoping to get home in time to read the kids a book. It was one of the few things he enjoyed doing and it was something they loved as well. Whenever he was working in his home office, they would always come in and say it was time for him to read a book, which he always did. His two kids were his driving force. He loved his family and he wanted to be able to provide for them and give them everything he had never had. They had a beautiful home. The school district was one of the best in the state and the children thrived. He and his wife drove new cars and did their best to keep up with the Joneses, the Smiths, and whoever else they were supposed to keep up with. Yet with this family also came great pressure and responsibility. Work hadn't been going so well and his last review was very troubling. His team was in disarray. Their productivity was in the toilet and George had been told that if he didn't get it together, he would be replaced. For the first time in his life his job was in serious jeopardy.

So as George walked, he thought of his family, his wife's ultimatum, and his job. He was in danger of losing it all, and the car problem was the final straw. Something good has to be coming my way, he thought. It can't continue like this or else I'm done. "My life wasn't always like this!" he shouted to the stars. "I was a young go-getter once. Everyone talked about my great potential. I was a rising star in my company. My future was bright. I squeezed the juice out of life. Now I can't even get my hands on a piece of fruit. I can't take this anymore!" he yelled. "Please help me!" he shouted as he looked up to the moonlit sky.

The air was silent and George heard nothing except the sound of his own breath. He was waiting for something. A word, a sound, a bolt of lightning. He wasn't sure what but something.

Chapter 4

George Wakes Up

George woke up the next morning feeling tired, anxious, and stressed as usual. Every day he wondered what else was going to go wrong, but at least today he knew he wouldn't have car problems. "Do you want me to drive you today?" his wife asked. "I do have time."

"No, it's okay," he answered. "I'll take the bus. It's not that bad. Except for the driver."

"What's wrong with the driver?" she asked.

"Long story, I'll tell you later," he said as he put on his sneakers for his trek to the bus stop. Then his mood turned even more sour as he thought about seeing the bus driver, who had insulted him. "Choose wisely; soap opera" stuck in his head. Who does she think she was talking to? He shook his head and then turned his attention toward his sneakers because it became painfully obvious that he wasn't able to untie his shoes. The laces were tied in 20 different knots, and he knew full well that his kids had been playing in his closet again. He threw his shoes against the wall, breathed a big huff, and just sat in painful silence.

More silence.

A minute later he looked in the mirror above his

dresser and saw himself as he heard a voice from his own conscience saying, "You, the bus driver was talking to you. You're the one with the failing marriage. You're the one who is about to get fired, who now doesn't even have a car to drive to work and can't even put on your own shoes. You're the one living a soap opera."

The realization hit him unexpectedly. He couldn't disagree with Joy. She was right. His life and career had hit rock bottom. Even his boss and biggest supporter and mentor had sat in his office yesterday and told him he couldn't vouch for him any more.

"I can't carry you, anymore," his boss said.

"I don't want to be carried," George replied.

"But that's what I've been doing. Everyone's asking me, what happened to George and I'm saying I don't know but he'll get it together. Well, now they are looking at me saying he better get it together or else you'll both be gone. I love you, George, like a son, but I can't let you bring me down, too. I've worked too hard for this. I have kids in college."

"I will get it together," George declared.

"We'll see," said his boss. "As my old football coach used to say, 'We don't talk this game, we play it.' So I hope to see action soon because if you don't get it together, then we both know what has to happen."

Fired was a word George never thought he would hear and now he was hearing it all too frequently in the same sentence with his name. I need to try to turn this around today, he thought. How? I have no idea.

Chapter 5

No Joy on the Bus

 George finally got his shoes on and as he walked to the bus stop, Joy the bus driver and her smile popped in to his head. Maybe she's not all that bad. After all, she pegged you, George, he thought to himself. But do I really need another person telling me how much my life stinks? I mean, not only do I have to hear it from my boss and my wife, but now I even have a bus driver and total stranger on me. Who would be next to tell me what a loser I am, the mailman?

He made it to the bus stop in plenty of time and waited for Bus #11 to pull up expecting to see Joy at the wheel, but when the bus arrived, Joy was nowhere to be found. Instead a man was at the wheel and he certainly didn't have the smile nor the welcome she had.

George wondered what had happened to her. He felt bad for being rude to her. After all, she was only trying to be nice and it wasn't her fault my life is in the toilet, he thought. George sat quietly on the bus. No conversation, no smiling, and certainly no energy. He thought about yesterday's meeting with his boss and the meeting he had with his team. He knew some changes had to happen and they had to happen quickly. He was ready to do something. What he wasn't sure but he knew he needed to do something to save his job, his family, and his marriage. He would start today, he thought.

Chapter 6

The Rules

 George arrived even earlier the next day at the bus stop. He sat on the bench and thought about work yesterday and how he had wanted to make an impact and get things moving in the right direction but as usual one crisis had led to another, and he and his team had spent most of the day dealing with conflict and putting out fires rather than getting something done. George thought about each member of his team and how each one contributed to his growing problems. I should fire every one of them. The thought made him smile but then reality set in and he knew there was no way he could do that. If anything he was the one who would be leaving the company before any of them. Besides, they weren't bad people. He had even hired a few of them. They had just lost their way somehow, he thought. Like a bad marriage, he figured, where you can't finger any one thing as the cause, yet you know it just isn't right. George was in such deep thought that he didn't hear Bus #11 pull up. When he looked up he saw Joy once again at the wheel and her smile made him smile.

"Weeellllll look aheeeeeerr. Look who we have here today. How you doing, Sugar? I didn't think I would see you again."

"Me neither," answered George. "I was on the bus yesterday, too, but you weren't here. Where were you?" he asked.

"Tuesday's my day off, Sugar. It's the day I take care of my sick father. He can't remember anything anymore. He doesn't remember his name nor his pride and joy. Could you imagine not being able to remember *me*! Not easy to see your father every week and he has no idea who you are."

"I'm sorry," said George, feeling bad that he hadn't thought she had a care in the world. Everything is not always as it seems.

"Don't be sorry, Sugar. It's part of life. Every one of us got challenges. Everyone who comes on this bus has problems. Some got marriage problems, health problems, family problems, work problems, and some got all kinds of problems. It's part of life and I'm just another person on the bus who's got another problem."

"But you're so happy and cheery," said George. "How do you stay so happy?"

"It's just what I'm all about, Sugar. It's because I love life. It's because I love you. And it's because I love me. How can I love myself if I don't love you? How could I love myself if I don't love everyone? You see we're all connected and I love it all. Even the ones who are hard to love."

Like me, George thought.

"Yes, like you, George," she said, reading his mind.

"And how about you?" she asked. "What are you doing on my bus again? I thought we had seen the last of
you after you ran off the bus faster than Carl Lewis at the
1984 Olympics. I consider myself blessed not once but
twice with your presence, so please do tell."

George told her about the flat tire, the repair shop,
the brakes, and how he could have crashed if he had dri-
ven the car and how he would have to take the bus for
about two weeks.

"Well, that's just great, George. The fact that you are
going to be riding on my bus is a great thing. As I said the
other day, you're on my bus for a reason. I didn't know
why exactly then but I do know now."

George asked why curiously, not quite catching on.
"What's so great about having your car in the shop for
two weeks?" he asked.

"Man, your head is hard to crack. But I'm going to be
gentle with you. Look up there, George, to the right of
the mirror. Tell me what you see."

"A sign," said George.

"That's right, a sign. And what does the sign say?"

"It says THE 10 RULES FOR THE RIDE OF YOUR LIFE." Underneath this headline was a list of 10 rules that George
couldn't really make out. He didn't have his reading
glasses on and the words were blurry. Besides the sign's
letters were handwritten and not very legible.

"That's right, Sugar. All my long-term passengers learn

these 10 rules. We talk about them often. And now I get to share them with you. I'm so excited!" she cheered.

"Look at the big picture here, George. This ain't no coincidence. We got about 10 days on my bus together and I got 10 rules for the ride of your life."

George squirmed a little in his seat. "I have enough rules in my life," he said. "Wife rules, home rules, Little League rules. The last thing I want is more rules."

Joy turned very serious for a moment. Her smile turned into a dead stare as she looked George right in the eye. "*You need these rules, George,*" she declared firmly. "Never turn your back on something that will change your life forever. You got 10 days and I got 10 rules that will change your life. Great things are coming your way if you're open, George. Be open. Please be open." And at that she smiled brightly once again and asked, "Are you with me?" in a calm, firm voice that made it clear she wasn't taking no for an answer.

"Yes," George answered, not believing he was actually agreeing to this.

And all at once the entire bus cheered, "Yes! Yes! Yes!" George looked around and for the first time realized that there were a group of other passengers on the bus as well.

"Don't be scared," Joy said. "We always chant Yes! when a new long-term passenger agrees to learn the 10 rules. It's our thing. It's what makes this the Energy Bus. We're all about positive energy here and it's what makes the ride so great. You don't get more positive than the word yes. So are you ready to learn rule #1? We've got five minutes before we get to your stop and this is a quick one."

George nodded, still in a little shock. Everything was moving really fast and a bunch of mixed feelings were swirling around inside him. On one hand he wanted to jump out the window, while on the other hand he was really curious to learn the 10 rules. After all, what did he have to lose? At this point nothing, he thought.

Chapter 7

You're the Driver

 "Rule #1 is easy," Joy declared as she turned to a man sitting opposite George. He looked like a combination of a well-dressed accountant and a mad scientist who could easily pass for Einstein's offspring.

"Danny, please show George rule #1," she asked. Danny reached into his large file folder sitting on his lap and pulled out a piece of paper that said:

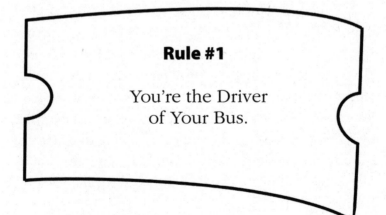

Rule #1

You're the Driver
of Your Bus.

Joy thanked Danny and shared how Danny had been made keeper of the rules. "A year ago he was what I call a Corporate Zombie," Joy explained. "Walking around with no purpose and no life. You could have hit him over the head with a sledge hammer and I don't think he would have noticed," she laughed. "Now he's keeper of the rules and helping us move the bus forward," she said proudly.

Taking a big swig from a large bottle of water that sat next to her seat, she turned her attention to George.

"Always remember that you are the driver of your bus. It's the most important of the rules because if you don't take responsibility for your life and control of your bus then you can't take it where you want to go. If you're not the driver, then you'll always be at the whim of every-one else's travel plans."

"But what about the support of others?" George asked.

"Of course you can seek directions and advice along the way, but remember it's your bus and your trip. We are all driving on each other's bus but each one of us has our own bus. The problem today," Joy continued, "is that people feel like they have no say where their bus is going or how it's going to get there. Tell them that stat about when the most people die, Marty," she directed as she looked in the rearview mirror at a young twentysomething man sitting toward the back of the bus.

He was dressed in a polo and khakis and had a

young face with blond hair that sat on his head like a mop. As Marty pulled out his laptop and starting keyboarding and clicking looking for the stat, Joy told George how Marty had come to be their research guy. How they would always get into interesting conversations about life, business, success, or whatever and like clockwork Marty would always come in the next day with some important research that shed some light on what they had discussed. They called him the Google Man because he could find the best information on any topic. "Here it is!" he shouted as he lifted up his laptop for everyone to see the screen. The screen read:

> ## MORE PEOPLE DIE MONDAY MORNING
> ## AT 9 A.M. THAN ANY OTHER TIME

"Isn't that amazing?" Joy asked George, who did not quite understand the significance of this research and just stood silent.

"Hello, George. I'm going to wake you up today like a shot of espresso," she chuckled. "Monday at 9 A.M. is when people start their workweek," Joy said passionately. "Think about that, George. People would rather die than go to work," she said as the passengers on the bus chuckled. "It sounds funny but actually it's quite sad. People feel like they don't have a choice. So they give up. But I am here to tell you today that you do have a choice. Right, folks?" she said rallying the passengers on the bus. "You don't have to sit passively by like so many other unhappy souls who let life create them. You can take the wheel and choose to create your life, one thought, one belief, one action, one choice at a time. It's your bus and you're the driver and you choose where you are going and the kind of ride it's going to be. Don't you agree, Sugar?" she asked.

"I don't know," George answered. "To me it feels like over time everyone in your life including life itself makes more and more decisions for you and before you know it, it's not even your life anymore. The government tells me what taxes I have to pay. My bosses tell me what to do at work. My wife orders me around at home. I feel imprisoned by my paycheck and responsibilities. So to answer your question, *no*, I really don't feel like I have a choice. The real truth is that instead of living, I feel like I'm dying every day. Maybe I'll be one of those 9 A.M. Monday morning people," George said.

"There's no maybe about it," Joy countered. "If you continue down this poor me road you are well on your way to being a Monday 9 A.M. fatality. So what you got to do now, George, is take the wheel and change direction. You may not have felt like you had a choice in the past, but starting now you will realize it's your greatest gift. And once you reclaim your power, everything and I mean everything will begin to change. No one can choose your attitude but you, George. No one else can choose your energy George. In fact, smile for me right now, Sugar." George didn't budge. "I'm not *asking* you, George. Now smile."

So he did, knowing she was one woman he didn't want to see get mad.

"See, George, you chose to smile and just by doing that one thing, you changed your energy. A smile changes the way you feel, the way you think, and how you interact with others. The energy you fuel the ride of your life with is entirely up to you. And as the driver, you are the one who must also choose your vision of where you want to go. You have the best seat and the best view of your life so it's up to you. You gotta have vision. So let me ask you, do you know where you want to go, George?"

George sat up straight, looked out the window, and noticed they were about a mile from his office building. He didn't have a clue where he wanted to go. He just knew he didn't want to be where he was anymore.

Joy had known it before George even thought it. A man with vision has a certain look in his eye and walk in his step. He walks like he knows where he is going and why he is going there, and George didn't walk like that. "I know we're almost at your office," Joy said, "but I want you to read something before you get off. It's something that inspired me to call this the Energy Bus. She reached into her bag next to her seat and pulled out a children's book with a graphical picture of a bus on the cover with the words *Energy Bus* on it.

"It's a children's book," George said, very frustrated as

29

he wondered why in the world she would want him to read a children's book right now.

"I know. That's what I love about it. You see, life is simple. But in all our stuff we make it complicated and become blinded to the simple truths. But it's the simplest lessons in life that are often the most profound and meaningful. So don't scoff at a children's book or the simple rules I share with you because one of the most important things you could ever realize is that *the closer you get to truth, the simpler and more powerful the lessons become.* Yes, the rules are simple but as you will realize they mean everything. So read, George. Read."

Feeling a little embarrassed, George started to read nonetheless and at once he was transported in his own mind to his house reading his children the book.

This is your energy bus.
You're the driver.
Did you know you can take your bus anywhere
*   you want to go?*
Say yes three times with me. Yes, yes, yes.
You can take it to the movies, the beach or the
*   North Pole.*
Just say where you want to go and believe that it
*   will be so.*
Because every journey and ride begins with a
*   desire to go somewhere and do something*
*   and if you have a desire then you also have*
*   the power to make it happen.*

The bus stopped and Joy turned to George. "So where do you desire to go, George? What's your vision?" she asked as she handed him a piece of paper. "Once you know this, all the other rules will fall into place."

George sat at his desk looking at the piece of paper Joy had given him.

At the top of the page were instructions from Joy: *First, decide what you want, George. Then you can start creating it. Don't let the world create you. You create your world. Complete these questions and we'll talk about them on the bus tomorrow.*

It had three sections on it with space for him to write and it looked like this.

1. My vision for my life (including my health) is

2. My vision for my work, career, job, and team is

3. My vision for my relationship and family is

Chapter 8

It's All About Energy

 When Bus #11 pulled up to George's bus stop the next morning, he watched a man run off the bus and then turn around and shout, "You're crazy, lady!"

"Oh yeah!" Joy shouted back. "When you are ready to learn something on my bus let me know."

"What was that all about?" George asked as he took his usual seat.

"He believes in the biggest illusion of our time," Joy answered. "Bigger than the illusion that the world is flat or that the sun moves east to west."

"Illusion," George paused. "What are you talking about?"

"The illusion that we live in a physical world," she declared with the confidence of a college professor. "You see, George, the universe is made of energy. Einstein taught us that."

Danny lifted up a piece of paper. "See, George, $E = MC^2$," he said.

Joy continued. "Einstein taught that anything that is

matter is energy so all the physical stuff we see and even our own bodies are really made of energy. So this is an energetic universe we live in and everything about us is energy. But you don't need to get deep and know anything about science to understand that life is all about energy," Joy said. "All you have to do is think about your own life. Think about the people who increase your energy and those who drain you. Think about the foods you eat that make you feel great and those that make you want to take a nap. Think about the projects at work that energize you and those that burn you out. Everything is energy. It is found in our thoughts, the words we say, the music we listen to, and the people who we surround ourselves with. Are you with me, George?"

"I am," answered George, who was thinking that he couldn't remember the last time anything at work had energized him."

"Watch professional football or basketball on television," she continued, "and you'll always hear the announcers talk about the energy of the team, the energy of a player, or the energy of the fans. Walk into any arena or stadium and you can feel the energy of the crowd. It's like there is electricity in the air. Coaches often talk about how their players are on the same wavelength or how the team is just out of synch. They'll also say things like, 'We're playing with a lot of energy tonight.' It's all about energy, George. Have you ever worked with a colleague and you both knew what each other was going to say next? Or you said the same thing at the same time?"

"Of course," George answered. "Happens all the time."

"Or has your wife ever read your mind?"

"Too many times," he said with a smirk.

"Energy of thought," she declared. "Our thoughts are powerful because they are loaded with energy. That's why I asked you to write down your vision for your life, work, and family," she said. "There is an energy to thought and when you identify what you desire and write down your vision, you begin the process of mobilizing the energy to create the life you want. After all you can't go somewhere if you don't have a vision of where you want to go. It's like trying to build a house without a set of plans and picture of what it's going to look like. It's like me driving this bus with no clue where my destination is. So George, please tell me you have a vision. Tell me where you want to go. I hope you wrote it down on the paper I gave you."

Chapter 9

George Shares His Vision

 George in fact did have a vision, several of them, and he had written them down. He pulled out the paper from his briefcase and explained to Joy that at first it had been a little hard to do this because it had been so long since he had thought about what he wanted. "I spend so much time living my life according to everyone's demands that it actually felt strange to think about what I want," he told her. "But once I got started it felt really good to think about what I want for my life."

She nodded, reassuring him with her big eyes and smile. "Go on, George. Do tell."

He told her about his vision for his personal life, how he had been a star college athlete who played lacrosse and how he wanted to get back into great shape and get rid of his big gut that hung over his belt. He explained how thinking about his vision made him remember a time in the past when he had been really happy and alive and how he wanted to feel that way again. He told Joy about wanting to be a better father and husband as well.

"I want my kids to look back 20 years from now and think of me as a happy, positive influence in their lives," he shared. "That's not the case now, so I know something has to change."

"What about your wife?" Joy asked. "What is your vision there?"

"I want my wife to stay married to me," he said. "I have this vision of us laughing together like we used to, remembering why we fell in love in the first place."

"Oh, you are such a romantic," Joy said, teasing him. She knew he had a good heart. She had liked him from the moment she had seen him get on her bus and had known buried underneath all those dark clouds was a light that wanted to shine. She was thrilled to see that light coming through as he shared his vision with her.

George, who was blushing now, however, didn't feel like a romantic at all. On the contrary he was petrified of losing his marriage, so he explained to Joy his situation and his hope that things would turn around.

"They will improve," Joy assured him but George didn't share her confidence.

"Just trust," she said calmly. "Trust."

Then she broached the subject of work and his vision for success at the NRG Company. George shared with Joy how he and his product marketing team had a big launch coming up for a new lightbulb called the NRG-2000. "If it doesn't go well I am toast. My career is done. So my vision is to somehow get my team on the same page and work really hard together to create and deliver a success-ful launch."

"On a scale of 1–10 how ready would you say you are for this product launch?" Joy asked.

"About 2," answered George. "We're disorganized, unmotivated, and quite frankly a sorry bunch."

"That's not good, Dude!" Marty shouted from the back of the bus.

"No, it's not good at all," George answered thinking that he wished the dude in the back of the bus would just be quiet.

Joy jumped into the conversation. "No, it's not good, George. But that don't mean it can't be good. It's not like we haven't faced crises before on my bus."

She looked at Marty. "Remember your rehab, Marty. And when Danny had that heart attack. What turned it all around was your desire and vision to change and the fo-cus to make it happen. Unfortunately, it takes a crisis for so many of us to change," she added. "I don't know why but it does. I wish more people wouldn't wait for every-thing to fall apart before they start thinking about their life and what they want. They don't have to wait, you know. But sometimes that's what it takes. *Sometimes we have to see what we don't want, to know what we do want.*"

As she was talking George thought of his mother with cancer and how she had told him all the changes she wanted to make when she survived, then he knew ex-actly what Joy was talking about.

"So yes, George," Joy continued, "this is your crisis but it's also your opportunity. Every crisis offers an opportunity to grow stronger and wiser; to reach deep within and discover a better you that will create a better outcome. So while this is your crisis, what matters most is what you do with it. Okay, so now that you know where you want to go and you have your desire and vision you are ready for rule #2."

Chapter 10

Focus

 Danny pulled out rule #2 on a piece of paper which said:

Rule #2

Desire, Vision, and Focus
Move Your Bus in the
Right Direction.

Joy turned around, looked at George, and said, "It's all about focus, George." Without focus buildings don't get built, paintings don't get painted, and energy gets scattered. You told us what you want. You shared your vision. Now I want to help you turn that vision into reality, and it all starts with thoughts."

41

"How are my thoughts going to make my work and marriage better?" George asked in a skeptical tone.

"The energy of thought as we discussed," Joy answered confidently. "Each day I want you to focus on your vision for 10 minutes and see yourself creating everything you wrote down on that paper. You see, Georgey, there is a law of energy."

"It's called the law of attraction!" Marty shouted from the back of the bus.

"That's right. The law of attraction," Joy continued, "and it says that the more we focus on something, the more we think about something, the more it shows up in our lives. For instance I bet every time you buy a new car you start seeing it everywhere on the road."

George nodded, knowing it was true.

"Ever wonder why that is?" Joy asked rhetorically. But before George could answer Joy said, "Because thoughts are magnetic. What we think about, we attract. What we think about expands and grows. What we put our energy and attention on starts to show up more in our life. And the energy we project through our thoughts is the energy we receive."

"That's why so many people have had the experience of thinking of a friend or relative and then they call on the phone," Marty confirmed. "The phenomenon actually has a scientific name. It's called *telephone telepathy*," he proudly shared, showing the research on his computer.

Joy continued. "There is an energy to thought. So it's important that you spend your time thinking about what you do want rather than what you don't want. You've got to focus. Do you know those people, George, who all they do is complain? They focus on what they don't want, don't like, and don't have."

"Of course I do," George answered, thinking to himself that he was one of them.

"Well, I tell those people that when you complain you get more things to complain about. So no more complaining and negativity, okay George? I don't allow complaining on my bus because if you are complaining you can't be thinking about or creating what you do want. Plus your complaining also ruins everyone else's ride.

I have a saying that I used to say on my school bus to the kids and now I even say it to my adult passengers as well because they often need to hear it more than the kids. It goes like this: *We're Winners, Not Whiners.*" With that the bus erupted in laughter and everyone started chanting, "We're winners, not whiners."

"So I want you to stop thinking about what you don't want and start focusing your energy on your vision and what you do want. Make sense, George?" Joy asked.

"The more you see it the more likely it will happen," Marty said from the back of the bus as he walked toward George to show him the research on visualization and Olympic athletes. "All the Olympic athletes use it because there's so much research that shows it works," Marty said. "Behind every gold medal are hours of visualizing their best performance or race. So why shouldn't dudes like you and I use it to create a phenomenal life and success?"

Marty knew this better than anyone else. He was one of those guys who never had had any luck until Joy showed him to create his own luck by projecting lucky energy. He was a surfer who dabbled in the Internet business, and he had just started a new company after selling his previous venture for several million dollars. Now he only expects good fortune and that's what he gets.

"We live in an Energy Field of Dreams!" Joy cheered. "If you build it in your mind, focus on seeing it, and take action, the success will come."

They were definitely making George think. His life was falling apart and maybe it was because of his negativity as his wife had told him so many times. He thought of himself at work and home and saw himself complaining a lot. But would changing these thoughts right now really make such a difference, he wondered. Would focusing on his vision really help attract it? He was an athlete and he had heard about athletes using visualization before but that's sports and this is life. A lot of negativity and problems had been accumulating for a long time and it had taken him a while to reach this crisis. Field of Dreams, right, he thought skeptically. Instead I'm building a big pile of you know what. Could he really turn it around that easily? But on the other hand, he didn't have a good reason not to try it. At this point he would try anything if it would mean saving his job and marriage. With a big product launch next Friday for the NRG-2000 this was a time for dreams because he had nothing else.

Chapter 11

The Power of Positive Energy

 "Okay, I'm on the bus," George said. "I've got my direction set and my vision is good. But I have to tell you, it's not so easy to think about what you want and be positive when you don't have a lot of things to be positive about and you keep getting what you don't want. You don't know the sharks I'm dealing with at work. You have no idea of the challenges I am facing right now. I'm hitting a lot of roadblocks."

"You're right, George," Joy answered. "I don't know all you are facing. But I do know that if you want to change your situation you must first change your thoughts. Because if you keep on thinking what you have been thinking you'll keep on getting what you have been getting. I also know this special formula I want to share with you. Show him, Danny." Danny reached into his briefcase and pulled out a paper sized sheet of cardboard. As George wondered how many signs he had in there, Danny lifted up the cardboard, which said:

$$E + P = O$$

"The E stands for events in your life," Danny explained. "The P stands for perception and the O stands for outcome. We can't control the events in our life but we can control how we perceive them and our perception and response to the events determine our outcome."

"The P can also stand for positive energy," Joy said, "and this formula explains why positive energy is so important. Sure, you have your vision for what you want to create in your life but there will always be people who don't share your vision. There will always be potholes and roadblocks that can block your journey on the road of life. Things happen like your flat tire, George. But it's how we choose to deal with the events in our life that means everything. We all get down but the key is what we do to turn life around. Like I told you, choose wisely. Positive energy and positive people create positive results. There is certainly a lot of negativity in the world and choosing positive energy helps us deal with the negative people and negative situations that can knock us off course.

"Positive energy helps keep the bus moving forward with momentum. And we're not talking about the fake kind of chest-thumping rah, rah positive energy that simply masks our negativity and annoys people. *No*, this is the real deal! We're talking about real positive energy that helps you overcome obstacles and challenges to create success. We're talking about trust, faith, enthusiasm, purpose, joy, and happiness. We're talking about the positive energy to inspire and lead others. We're talking about the positive energy that makes you feel great instead of the negative energy that drains you. This is the real stuff, my man, and it's the key to life and rule #3. Show him, Danny."

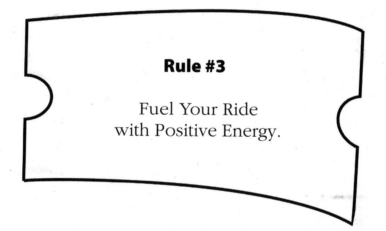

Rule #3

Fuel Your Ride
with Positive Energy.

"Think of it like this, George," Joy continued. "Desire, vision, and focus help you turn the bus in the right direction but positive energy is necessary to take you where you want to go. Every day when we look at the gas pump of life we have a choice between positive energy and negative energy. Positive energy is high octane fuel for the ride of your life while negative energy causes sludge to accumulate in your energy pipeline."

"But what do I do with the negativity I have?" asked George.

Joy pointed to the trash bucket. "Right there, George. You let it go. You release it. You throw it out. You transform it. When the work is piled high on your desk, think about how thankful you are to even have a job while so many are unemployed. When work is driving you crazy, think about the fact that you are healthy enough to work. When you are sitting in traffic, be thankful you can drive a car while so many have to walk miles just to get clean water. When the restaurant messes up your meal, think about how many unfed mouths there are in the world. And as I told my father a number of years ago when he lost the love of his life—my mother, 'You had the kind of love for so many years that many people spend a lifetime searching for and never find. Let's be thankful for that.' "

Joy added, "Where there is a negative there is always a positive. Where there is a dark cloud, there is always a sun shining behind it."

"So you're saying that I need to keep fueling my life with positive energy if I want to be successful," George asked.

"I'm not saying it," Joy answered. "I'm screaming it! I have found that where there is a void, negativity will fill it so we must keep fueling up with positive energy so the negative energy doesn't have room to expand. We must fuel up daily with positive thoughts, cultivate positive feelings, and take positive actions. Positive energy is all of these things. Without it your ride will stall."

The Energy Bus

"And what about my team at work?" George asked.

"Same thing," Joy answered. "We'll need to get them focused and positive, too. You'll want them to understand and be a part of your vision. You'll want to get 'em on the bus. I've got some rules for you that are going to make them big-time successes but we're not ready for that yet. First, let's help you fuel up with positive energy because you can't share the positive energy if you don't have it yourself. Once you get your bus rolling then you'll be ready to ask your team to get on. One mile at a time, my man. One positive thought, feeling, and action at a time. We'll talk about your team soon."

As the bus approached George's stop, Joy directed Marty to pull out what she called That Energy Book and read him the story about the positive dog. Marty picked up the book that was sitting next to him and started reading.

A man goes to the village to visit the wise man and he says to the wise man, "I feel like there are two dogs inside me. One dog is this positive, loving, kind, and gentle dog and then I have this angry, mean-spirited, and negative dog and they fight all the time. I don't know which is going to win." The wise man thinks for a moment and he says, "I know which is going to win. The one you feed the most, so feed the positive dog."

"Thank you, Marty," Joy said as she directed him to give George the book.

"I can't," said George. "It's yours."

"No, it's yours," said Marty. "We give them away all

the time on the bus so consider it a gift of energy. Instead of you swimming against the current of life, this book will help you ride some awesome energy waves."

"That's right," said Joy. "This book is going to help you take action and feed the positive dog inside you so you cultivate the positive energy you need to succeed. It's pretty simple. Just do one of the 10-minute exercises in the book. Pick any one you want. Just do one today and feel your energy rise."

"I will," George said. "I'm ready to take action."

As George walked off the bus and toward his building Joy shouted, "Feed the positive dog, George! Feed the positive dog!"

He looked back and pumped his fist in the air as he walked to work, but then he realized he was walking into a building where his future couldn't be more negative.

Chapter 12

George Takes a Walk

 As George sat at his desk thumbing through the book Marty had given him looking for a positive energy exercise that appealed to him, he thought of his old friend Chuck who had made a fortune during the Internet boom. He remembered how surprised he had been to hear that Chuck and his wife had divorced. He thought about appearances and how on the outside Chuck seemed to have everything. Money. Family. Big house. A plethora of companies that wanted Chuck to run them. Yet George realized everything isn't always what they seem. He found out that Chuck really had a lot of personal problems that spilled over and caused the destruction of everything else in his life. When George really thought about it, he never remembered Chuck being happy.

Thinking of Chuck made him realize even more than ever that he didn't want to go down that road. Everyone else probably thought they had it all, too. If they only knew, he thought. Appearances weren't enough. The show wasn't doing it anymore. He wanted to feel good, so a big smile came across his face when he came across the Thank-You Walk in the Energy Book. One moment he was reading how it's physically impossible to be stressed and thankful at the same moment, and the next minute he was walking around his building outside saying what he was grateful for.

He knew if people from his company saw him talking to himself they would think he was crazy but he didn't mind. Sure it felt a little funny but the walk was energizing him, and counting his blessings really did make him feel great. The book said that being grateful floods the body and brain with positive endorphins and emotions and combined with walking is a powerful energy booster. It sure was right. As George walked back into his building he felt more positive, energized, and ready to take on the day at work. Joy was right, he thought. Feeding the positive dog does feel good. Now if I can just feed the lions at work I'll be okay. He chuckled as he walked into his office to meet with his team about the new product launch.

Chapter 13

One Great Golf Shot Theory

 That night while watching television George acted on an inspired impulse to go grab his bag and pull out the Energy Book Marty had given him. As he looked through it, one section really caught his attention. It was about golf, a sport he loved to play but rarely had time for. The book talked about how after people play a round of golf they usually don't think about all the bad shots they made but rather always remember and focus on the one great shot they had that day. The thought and feeling they get when thinking about this shot makes them want to play again and again; this is why so many people get addicted to golf. The book then contrasted this with life and how people often go to bed thinking about all the things that went wrong when instead they should apply the one great golf shot theory to their life and think about the one great thing that happened that day. The one great call, meeting, or sale; the one great conversation or interaction; the one great success that will inspire them to look forward to creating more success tomorrow. This, the book said, will inspire people to get addicted to life.

Well, it worked because George was inspired. He had an idea, walked into his children's bedrooms and asked each one to tell him their success of the day. He explained that it could be something great that had happened to them that day or something they were proud of. The children lit up and smiled as they recalled their successes and George knew this would be their new nightly ritual.

Then he took a walk around the block with his dog and thought about his own success that day. His boss had come up to him and said, "There's something different about you, George. Whatever you are doing, keep it up." It's amazing how positive energy works, George thought. Whether you have it or don't, people notice.

Later on that night as he lay his head on the pillow George thought about sharing the one great golf shot theory with his team because if there was any group of people on the planet who needed to learn to focus more on the positive instead of the negative, it was they.

Chapter 14

Bus Tickets

 It was Friday and everyone loves Fridays. Today George loved Friday more than ever. Today he hopped onto Bus #11 like a new man.

"What's gotten into you, Sugar?" Joy asked as she gave him a big smile.

"I don't know. I guess it's the Thank-You Walk I did on the way to the bus stop," George said. "I did one at work yesterday, too, and a success walk last night. It really seems to work."

"I told you, George. There's nothing better than feeding the positive dog. But listen here. I got something real important to tell you. Me and the team have been talking and we have decided that we really want to help you succeed with that new lightbulb you are introducing. So now that you've got the positive energy flowing you're ready to share it with your team which is a good thing because if you want to have a successful product launch you're going to need to get your team on your bus. So this is rule #4, George. Show him, Danny." Danny pulled out rule #4, which said:

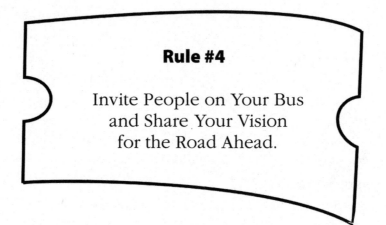

Rule #4

Invite People on Your Bus
and Share Your Vision
for the Road Ahead.

"Remember, you're driving the bus, George," Joy said. "But as you drive you want to keep asking people to get on. The worst they can say is no. If you don't ask they won't know to get on. Plus, the more people you pick up along the way the more energy you create during your ride. The goal is to eventually have a standing room only bus and since this is an energy bus it is always expanding so you'll always be able to add more people. Now that you know this, George, it's important that you ask your team to get on your bus or else you'll be driving the product launch by yourself and you can't do this one alone. You need your team to make this work. Are you getting what I'm saying?" she asked.

"Yes, I am," George answered as he thought of his team in disarray. He knew there was too much to do to launch it by himself and he knew only an organized, energized team could deliver a successful product launch. But what he didn't know was how to make this happen. "What did you have in mind?" he asked.

"Ohhh have we got the ticket, George. We got the ticket literally," Joy said as she took a big swig from her water bottle.

"Do you want me to explain it to him?" a petite woman with brown, grayish hair said politely as she sat upright in her seat.

"Sure," answered Joy, "but first let me tell George who you are." Joy explained that Janice was a teacher at a local school and she has been sharing the energy bus rules with her teachers and students for a while with great success, so much success that she launched a web site www.theenergybus.com to share the rules with the world so everyone could benefit.

"Can you believe that, George!" Joy exclaimed. "We're global now and Janice is bringing our message to people around the world."

"It's very exciting," Janice said timidly joining the conversation, "and because Joy explained how important it is for people to build their team with positive people who support them in their endeavors, I decided to add a feature to the web site that allows someone like you and me to send an e-bus ticket via e-mail to invite their friends, co-workers, bosses, family, or whomever to get on their bus. At the web site you can also print out tickets to personally hand to people if you want to invite them face to face."

"Isn't that fantastic, George?" Joy said to him as she gave a big thumbs up to Janice.

Janice spoke up again. "Oh and I almost forgot. We also made it possible for you to write a message that is e-mailed along with your e-bus ticket explaining your vision and goal. So when you send your e-bus tickets to your team George, you can say *This is my vision for our team and our product launch and this is where my bus is going and I want to invite you to get on.* We do this often at school when we are starting new initiatives, and the principal sends an e-bus ticket to all the teachers inviting them to get on her bus. It's a lot of fun but more importantly it works."

"That's what I'm talking about!" Joy said, more excited than ever. "There's no better way to get people on your bus than telling them where you are going and asking them to get on. But remember, George, you must share your vision with them. You must make it clear what you expect the launch to be like and how you expect the team to work together with no infighting and no egos getting in the way. And tell them how you expect everyone to come together for the collective good of delivering a stellar performance. If you don't clearly communicate your vision of the road ahead no one will want to travel with you."

Joy then advised George on a plan of action. She had been through this drill before and it had worked wonders with everyone who had ever come on her bus. It even worked before they had a fancy web site and had to make the tickets by hand. But they were equipped and now George would be, too. She told him how he should e-mail an e-bus ticket, without a message, to his boss and his team at work. That would get them curious, she told him. She took him step-by-step and explained how to meet individually with each person, share his vision for the product launch, and give each person a paper bus ticket printed from www.theenergybus.com. Then she advised him to conclude with, "Now that you know where my bus is going and you are clear about my vision for the road ahead, if you are ready to get on my bus then return the ticket with your name on it to my office Monday morning by 9 A.M."

George was looking forward to making this happen. Timing couldn't be better since the launch of the NRG-2000 was a week from today and on Monday he would know who was on his bus and who wasn't. Plus the weekend would give everyone time to prepare for the upcoming big week. The energy is shifting, he thought.

"Oh and one more thing," Joy said as the bus reached George's office building. "Make sure you do a separate e-bus ticket for your wife, too, and tell her your vision for yourself, your marriage, and your family. She needs to know where you want to go, George. Don't forget that."

Bus Tickets

"I won't," George replied. "I'll do just that." For the first time he was thankful that his car had had a flat tire. Maybe everything does happen for a reason, he thought. Maybe for the first time in a long while luck is smiling on me and maybe just maybe this means my luck and situation are about to improve.

Chapter 15

A Very Long Weekend

 While George was pacing around his bedroom he noticed a *Time* magazine sitting on his nightstand with Abraham Lincoln on the cover. George was fascinated with the life and presidency of Abraham Lincoln. He marveled that this man who was said to suffer from depression was able to overcome several election defeats, two bankruptcies, a nervous breakdown, and the death of his fiancée before becoming President of the United States. A seeming failure at the age of 51, he had summoned the courage and strength that unified our country and changed the course of history. George couldn't help but imagine what it must have been like in the past for Lincoln to wait and wait and wait for the Civil War battle reports to come in, not knowing if his country was one step closer to unification or destruction.

Yet now as George spent time with his family and did chores around the house he had a small sense of what it was like to wait and wait and have your fate unfold before you. As time inched slowly by, he continually wondered who was going to be on his bus and who would stay off it. He wondered if he had the strength and courage to overcome his own small civil war at work. And he wondered if he was headed toward victory or defeat. He had handed out the bus tickets on Friday and he felt great about his meetings, but Monday would be the telling point. He walked over to his bookshelf, pulled out his favorite Abraham Lincoln book, and randomly flipped through it only to find a quote that jumped out at him and would bring him a newfound resolve.

> *I am not bound to win, I am bound to be true.*
> *I am not bound to succeed, but I am bound to live up to the light that I have.*
>
> —Abraham Lincoln
> sixteenth President of the United States of America

Chapter 16

Who's on the Bus

 It was Monday and this Monday was very different from last Monday. Instead of dread George felt a nervous excitement.

He had taken an earlier bus to work today so he could be in his office in time to receive the bus tickets from his new passengers. He greeted each person as they walked, one by one, into his office, handed in their tickets, and told him they were on his bus. All of them except Michael, Jamie, and José. The three of them walked in together, and immediately George knew something was up. He could tell they were nervous and that they weren't holding bus tickets. I bet they are too scared to come in alone so they decided to pack together like a bunch of wolves, he thought.

"We think your bus is going to crash and we don't want to be on it when it does," Michael bluntly told him.

"We need this job," Jamie said nervously.

"Who's we?" George asked.

"All of us," they said in unison as they looked around at each other.

"Your bus is going to go up in flames," Michael said.

The words hit George like a dagger in the heart. Michael and Jamie always had given him problems and he expected they wouldn't get on his bus. But José was a big surprise. José had always worked hard for him. And the biggest surprise of all was that José chose to stay off the bus while Larry and Tom, the two biggest problems of all, handed in their tickets and decided to get on.

As the three wolves stood there, George didn't know what else to say. He was in shock. Sure, he had contemplated that there might be people who wouldn't get on his bus but he never thought what he would do if this actually happened. Now it was staring him right in the face and he felt lost.

"Thank you," is all George said as they walked out of his office and he slumped into his chair.

Thinking about his team dynamics he felt more hopeless than ever. Two people he thought would surely stay off his bus wanted to be on it, and the one person he had thought would be his first passenger said no.

Needless to say the day did not go well. Larry and Tom continued causing problems by fighting with each other and the rest of the team. They complained about everything and bashed other people's ideas while offering no solutions of their own. George tried to get everyone on the same page but he was severely distracted by the three wolves who did not want to get on his bus. He didn't know what he should do with them so he just let them sit there passively at the meetings as they let everyone else know how they felt by rolling their condescending eyes at each other.

The energy felt horrible and so did George. They had four days until the launch and his bus was stalled.

Chapter 17

The Enemy Is Negativity

 Tuesday morning George walked on the bus with no life and certainly no kick in his step. He felt like a failure and was embarrassed to face the people who were trying so hard to help him succeed. Joy read his energy immediately and knew things had not gone well for him at work. This was her day off and the day she usually visited her father but she had a feeling George would need her today and wanted to be on the bus to share some energy and lift him up if he needed it. Now as she looked at George she was sure glad she had followed her hunch. It wasn't the first time she had seen the look of defeat. In fact, most people she recalled had setbacks as they learned how to drive their bus. Every person and every team will be tested on their journey. It was part of the curriculum of life. She knew this all too well. It's just like riding a bicycle, she thought. In the beginning you're going to fall off and get knocked down but the important thing is to get back on, stay strong, and after a while once you master it you'll ride with the confidence of a champion. She just had to help George take the wheel and quick because he was running out of time.

"What's the matter, Sugar?" she asked. "Where's the George who sprang on my bus on Friday?"

"He's been knocked down by two left jabs and a right hook," answered George.

"Well, it's time to get back up!" Joy exclaimed. "Life is always going to knock you down. The important thing is you got to get back up. Haven't you seen the movie *Rocky?*" she asked. Her words piqued his interest. He had always loved the original *Rocky* movie and had even written his college essay about the movie and a person overcoming their demons and challenges to become someone of worth and value.

"Well, of course I have. Who hasn't?" he said. "But that's a movie," he said skeptically.

"And this is life, George, and I'm telling you to get back up," she said sternly.

"But I failed," he said.

"You haven't failed until you stop trying, George. Now pick that sorry head of yours up, sit up straight, and let's talk about how to build some mental and emotional muscle and get your bus rolling."

Joy asked George what had happened that got him so down and he explained the situation and team dynamics to her. He cursed his two biggest problems, Larry and Tom, and the three wolves who had sabotaged him all day.

"They're not the problem," Joy said to his surprise.

"What's the problem then?" George asked, feeling annoyed.

"Negativity itself," she said. "You see there will always be negativity everywhere and in everything you do, George. You will always be surrounded by negative people. It's not these people so to speak. It's the negativity they represent. They are just one of many you will come across."

Marty stood up and shouted from the back with more of his beneficial research. "And the Gallup Poll estimates that there are 22 million negative workers in the United States costing around $300 billion in productivity a year!"

"And this negativity not only kills productivity and companies, George, it also kills people. Self-doubt, fear, hopelessness, and negative energy drain you and sabotage everything you want in life and all the success you desire," Joy added. "So the same negativity these people represent is also inside you. That's why you got to feed the positive dog, George."

"But I have these negative people on my bus. And a few other negative people who didn't want to get on my bus. Are you saying I'm the problem and that they are not the problem?" George asked. "I'm quite frankly a little confused."

"Listen, George, you are too close to the problem to see it. The problem is that you are taking it too personal. Step back for a moment. Don't focus on these people personally. Forget they even have names. Don't think of it as you versus them. Just realize that they represent the

The Enemy Is Negativity

negativity that will always be around you. The important thing is to know how to deal with the negativity and what to do with it.

"So let's first deal with the negative people who didn't get on your bus," Joy said. "Show him rule #5, Danny." Danny lifted up the sign, which said:

Rule #5

Don't Waste Your Energy
on Those Who Don't
Get on Your Bus.

"It's simple, my man. Some people are going to get on your bus and some people won't. Don't worry about the people who don't get on your bus. Don't waste your energy on them. Don't try to make them get on. You can't drive anyone else's bus. You can only drive your bus."

"I know what you mean," George said. "I tried to drive my wife's bus for a few years and I quickly learned that she doesn't like it when I try to drive her bus." The passengers on the bus chuckled as Joy continued sharing her energy gospel.

"That's right, George. Everyone has to make their own choices and you have to make yours. And certainly don't spend your energy being upset that these people didn't get on your bus. Don't take it personal. Maybe they are meant to get on another bus. Maybe if they got on your bus they would ruin your ride." George knew this would definitely be the case.

"Plus, the more energy you spend worrying about the people who didn't get on your bus, the less you will have for the people who are on your bus. And if you are worrying about the people who didn't get on your bus you won't have the energy to keep on asking new people to get on. Salespeople know this real well, George. If they get caught up in rejection they lose the energy to go after new customers and ask new people to get on their bus. So for the people who don't get on your bus just let them sit at the station as you drive on by."

George now realized the grave mistake he had made. He had spent so much time thinking about the three wolves that he had completely ignored the people who wanted to be on his bus. He had been so tired and drained that he had no energy to move the bus forward.

"But what about the people who get on your bus but are really negative?" George asked as he thought of Tom and Larry. The mere thought of them sent shivers down his spine.

Joy would have an answer for them as well and the solution didn't require weapons or garlic.

Chapter 18

No Energy Vampires on the Bus

 "You asked about the negative people and I'm going to be straight up with you, George. This rule is not for the faint of heart. It's not easy to deal with the negativity in the world but it's something that's got to be done. Your success and life are so important that you must surround yourself with a positive support team. No one creates success in a vacuum and the people we surround ourselves with have a big influence on the life and success we create. If you want to be successful you have to be very careful about who is on your bus. After all there are people who increase your energy and there are people who drain your energy. I call the people who drain your energy Energy Vampires and they will suck the life out of you and your goals and vision if you let them. They will cause an engine leak, make your ride miserable, or even worse slash your tires. But remember, George, don't take it personal. They are just part of the negativity that exists in the world. Your job is to do your best to eliminate any negativity on your bus and this includes negative people, no matter who they are. This is rule #6 and it's big time. Show him, Danny."

Rule #6

Post a Sign That Says
NO ENERGY VAMPIRES ALLOWED
on Your Bus.

"You got to be strong enough to tell people that you will not allow any negativity on your bus. You got to say this is where we are going and to get there we need a positive and supportive team and whoever is negative will be kicked off the bus or left at the station.

As Joy spoke George envisioned Larry, Tom, Michael, José, and Jamie all sitting at the bus station as his bus drove off and he had to admit it felt very good. But could he really kick people off his bus? And what about the three wolves? He couldn't possibly banish them, could he? Before he could ask Joy she said, "Those two Energy Vampires, Tom and Larry, you need to have a meeting with them first thing today and say "Look, I don't allow any negativity on my bus. If you are not going to be positive and contribute to our vision then you're off the bus and you'll have to look for another job."

"That's tough," George said.

"I know it is, Sugar, but sometimes it's what's got to be done. You give people a chance to change and if they don't get it then you got to kick them off the bus. Or else they will ruin your ride."

"What about the three wolves who chose to stay off my bus in the first place?" asked George. "What should I do with them?"

"Meet with them, too," Joy answered. "Tell each one that they have one more opportunity to get on your bus. If they don't accept your invitation then make them sit at their desks by themselves while you and your team have your meetings. Don't include them in anything. After the product launch you can figure out a future plan of action with your human resources folks."

George liked what he had heard and he was ready to take action. He felt equipped with the tools to handle the Energy Vampires and unite his team to succeed. He wondered, however, why he had never learned any of this in his management training classes. They teach all these policies and procedures, he thought, but they never help us deal with real people and real problems.

Chapter 19

The Ultimate Rule
of Positive Energy

 As they approached George's office, Joy gave him one last piece of important advice. "There's one last thing I got to tell you about all this, George, you really need to know. It's so important it's not even part of the 10 rules. It's in a class all by itself. It's like the ultimate rule of positive energy. And it's so important I want you to write it down."

George pulled out a piece of paper and a pen and waited for Joy to continue. "Here it is, George. *Your positive energy and vision must be greater than anyone's and everyone's negativity. Your certainty must be greater than everyone's doubt.* After all, George, there will always be people who don't share your vision. There will always be the doubters who doubt, doubt, and doubt and tell you you can't do this and you won't be able to accomplish that. They think that dreams were meant for others but not for people like you and them. And there will even be people who don't want you to succeed because it makes them see their own weaknesses and failures. Rather than driving their own bus they are trying to ruin everyone else's ride.

"So that's how important your positive energy is, George. You can always kick people off your bus and you'll need to do that from time to time but just remember that there will always be more negative people who get on. And sometimes you will have an Energy Vampire on your bus like a boss or someone who you can't kick off. You got to deal with them. That's why you got to feed the positive dog and why you got to cultivate it every day and why we gave you the Energy Book.

"One day is not enough, George. It's got to be a habit. Positive energy is like muscle. The more you use it the stronger it gets. The stronger it gets the more powerful you become. Repetition is the key and the more you focus on positive energy the more it becomes your natural state. So when someone comes at you with negativity you will be able to respond with strength and positive energy. Just as you become a more skilled golfer by playing more often you also develop the skill of positive energy by practicing. The more you do it the more natural it becomes. So grow it and build it so you have the power to overcome the negativity. That's how it works, George. That's the key."

George couldn't argue with her. His positive energy wasn't that powerful. That's why he had been so shaken by the people who hadn't gotten on his bus. He didn't have that strength and certainty and his vision wasn't focused. He had allowed himself to be manipulated and affected by the naysayers because he was weak. He knew today would be the day that they would have to get the bus moving. Because it was up to him, and he had to be strong, he vowed to himself that today would be different. But before he could step off the bus, Joy grabbed his arm.

"Oh, and one more thing before you leave, George. Take this rock."

"What is it?" George asked as he held out his hand.

"Well, I know it doesn't look like much all black and dirty, pretty ugly actually, but it's a special rock that was given to me by my teacher. When he gave it to me he said, "Find the value in this rock and you will find a priceless treasure inside yourself and in all the people you encounter."

"What do I do with it?" George asked.

"Put it in your pocket for now," she said, "and then look at it often and let it remind you of what I just told you. Find the value in yourself. Find it in the rock. Find it in your team."

Chapter 20

George Takes Control of His Bus

 The first thing George did when he got to his office was call Larry in for a meeting. He wanted to meet with each Energy Vampire, as Joy suggested, so he could get his bus rolling first thing in the morning. He knew he needed to take action and fast. The team was waiting and they needed serious direction, focus, and positive energy today.

As he sat at his desk waiting for Larry to walk in, a feeling of fear and nervous energy enveloped him. It feels like game day, he thought as he remembered what it had felt like to have a nervous feeling in the pit of his stomach before his big lacrosse games. With the crowds cheering and the anticipation building he remembered feeling like he was going to collapse and yet explode with excitement at the same time. He knew this feeling well and it was good. It made him feel alive and let him know he was ready. Plus his nervous energy had often become fuel for some of his best performances. It's game day, he thought and for the first time in a long time he felt alive and ready.

As soon as Larry walked in and before he could make a negative comment to George for interrupting his creative thought process, George struck hard and fast. He told Larry point blank that he had had enough of Larry's negativity and if he didn't help move the bus forward in a positive manner, then he was off the bus, effective immediately. Larry, while in shock at George's directness, responded with willingness and agreed to George's demands for positive energy and positive contribution. George wasn't surprised. He knew Larry had a family and couldn't afford to lose his job right now.

Tom, on the other hand, was a completely different case. He had no allegiances to anyone especially to George. They had never liked each other and they both knew it. But this isn't a matter of liking each other, George thought. It is a matter of getting things done and having the right team in place for the NRG-2000 product launch. So when Tom walked in, George was ready.

"I want you on my team, Tom. But I can't have you on the team if you are going to prevent us from achieving our goals," George said. "I can't have you be a disruptive influence anymore."

"Who are you kidding?" Tom responded forcefully. "The only disruptive influence is you. The problems we are having are not because of me. They are because you can't lead. Don't blame me. Blame yourself. I know we don't like each other, never have, but the real problem is that I don't respect you as a leader, and I'm certainly not going to say what you want me to say so I can go on your silly little ride with you. You need me, George. The team needs me and if you get rid of me now, then you'll be driving your bus right off a cliff. So unless you have something important to say to me, I'd like to get back to doing my job."

George's shoulders slumped forward. He could feel his body getting weak as if the energy was being sucked out of him. He was wilting like a dying plant. He didn't know what to say and was shaking from head to toe. "So why did you hand in your bus ticket?" George asked.

"I only handed my bus ticket in to you because I want a front row seat when I watch your bus implode," Tom said with a big grin on his face. "You and I both know it's going to happen and when it does no one will be happier than me."

George put his hand passively into his pocket and felt the rock that Joy had given him. He took it out and looked at it as he tried to think of what to say next. He had never expected to be overtaken like this.

"What is that?" Tom asked. "Your pet rock?"

As George looked at the rock he remembered what Joy had said about finding the value in yourself. He realized Tom didn't believe in him because George didn't believe in himself. He was allowing himself to be pounced on and verbally assaulted by a grinning, arrogant, Energy Vampire who had no interest in helping his team succeed and certainly no desire to help George turn things around. And worst of all he was taking it, just as he had taken it the past few years from everyone and everything.

Every day life had beaten him down a little more. Each day his confidence had shrunk. And each moment he became less of the person he admired and more of the person he pitied. George vowed he would not be weak today. He had vowed he would be strong, yet here he was being weak and beaten down again. Enough, George thought to himself as he clenched the rock in his fist. Enough, he thought as the word echoed throughout his entire body. Tom took a step back as he saw a transformation come over George.

No longer will I become a punching bag for life or anyone else for that matter, George thought as he took a step toward Tom. "You think I'm just going to sit here and let you talk to me like this?" George said. Before Tom could answer, George said, "Think again. Are you very talented? Of course you are. Could we use you for this product launch? You bet. But I'd rather have less talent and a team that is all moving in the same direction and striving for the same goals than a team with someone who has your attitude. So guess what, Tom. If the bus blows up, you won't have to worry because you won't be on it. Effective immediately you are off the bus. I didn't want it to be this way but what you just said to me and your attitude give me no other choice. You are fired." Tom's jaw dropped as he stood frozen in shock. Then he turned, walked out of the office without saying a word, and slammed the door shut.

One Energy Vampire off the bus, George thought as he stood there still shaking from the argument. It wasn't easy but he knew it was the right decision. Even though Tom was one of his most talented people, which is why he had put up with Tom for so long, it had to be done and the team would be better off for it. Personally George felt like a 200 pound weight had been lifted off his shoulders. He felt strong and free. Looking at the rock one more time before putting it into his pocket, he thought of Joy and smiled. For the first time in a long time he was proud of himself.

George's plan for the three wolves included Joy's recommendation of simply isolating them from the team since they didn't want to be on the bus. But when Michael walked into his office with guns blazing telling George that he was crazy for firing Tom and that this surely meant the bus was going up in flames and so was George, he had no other choice but to tell Michael it was this bus's way or the highway. Michael, too proud to succumb and too angry to retreat, quit and decided he would get on another bus traveling on another road. That makes two, George thought.

After the fireworks show George had experienced this morning he wondered what else could be next. He didn't like conflict, fighting, or yelling. He certainly didn't like firing people or losing two members of his team. But he had vowed to stay strong and true to his vision. It was either this or failure. He was ready for battle with Jamie and José but truly hoped they wouldn't have to exchange blows.

When George told Jamie she was either on his bus or off it, she agreed to be on it but then hit him, not with

85

George Takes Control of His Bus

negativity but with the hard truth. "I've worked for you for several years now, George," she said. "And every year, every day for that matter, you seem to get grumpier and more bitter. We even had bets about when you would just implode, not show up one day, and give up. But every day you kept coming in making yourself miserable and your team miserable in the process. This team is a shambles not because of us, but because of you. None of us could believe they kept you so long. And so when you told us you wanted us to get on your bus, I'm like there is no way I'm getting on his bus. Why should I, when his bus has been trudging along aimlessly for the past year? But if you say I have to get on my bus to keep my job, I will. I'll get on it but I want you to know why I didn't get on it in the first place."

George sat there stunned. He knew everything she had said was true and yet it was difficult to accept it. He didn't know what to say or how to respond. He wanted to tell her about Joy, the Energy Bus, and what he had learned but he was paralyzed, and besides he didn't have time to get into it. All he did was thank her for her honesty and for being on his bus and wait for José, who was about to deliver another blow.

When José walked in, George immediately said he was surprised that José didn't want to get on his bus after all they had done together. José didn't pull any punches either and came right back.

"That's right, George," he said. "I've given you my all. I've done everything you asked me to do. I stay late, I work weekends, I pick up everyone else's slack, and not once do you say thank you. Not once do you tell me that you appreciate my hard work and loyalty. When I asked you for a raise you said you would think about it and never talked about it again to me. What's that all about, George? You just walk around here worrying about you and your job, and you don't really care about me. So when you all of a sudden ask me to get on your bus because you want to save your job, and don't think we don't know that if this launch fails you are gone because everyone knows that, I'm supposed to get all excited and go, 'Whoopeeeeeeeeee I'm on the bus.' It's not happening. It's hard for me to get on your bus when you surely haven't been on mine!" he shouted.

Once again George was hit right between the eyes. He had been taking a lot of blows lately and this one coming from the person he liked and trusted the most was the hardest. But he knew José was right and there was nothing he could say to make José feel better at this moment. He was fired up and George understood why.

"You're right," George said. "You are right. That's all I can say."

José, who was expecting to get fired, was surprised at George's response. He had seen Michael and Tom walk out of the office earlier and thought everyone was getting fired, so he was stunned and relieved at the same time that George was acting so calm. For a few moments George and José stood there in awkward silence, both not knowing what to say.

87

George Takes Control of His Bus

José spoke first. "Okay, now what?" he asked.

George stood silent considering "now what" as a thought popped into his head that said, You can't change the past. Let it go. Create the future.

"Now we create our future," George answered confidently as his eyes lit up. He had been knocked to the canvas again with two right hooks, but this time he got up. He wasn't giving up this time. No, this time he was charging forward toward his vision. "Now I ask you to give me a chance to make it up to you," he said. "I don't know how yet but I'll think of something. Just please help me with the launch and let me prove to you that I'm someone you feel good about working for. Let me show you I'm here for you." José agreed and they walked out of his office together to gather the team for a meeting that would be the start of a very productive and positive day.

Chapter 21

George Has a Dream

That night after one of the most productive days at work George had experienced in years, he had a dream. He was driving a bus and on it were his employees, his wife, and his children. The bus was racing down the mountain toward a big black hole in the ground. Just as the bus was about to crash and explode, an invisible hand lifted the bus, George, and all his passengers to safety. Then as George, his team, and his family stood on a ledge overlooking the abyss an incredible feeling of peace came over him, and he heard a whisper call out to him, "Trust that great things are happening." He had woken up in a deep sweat thinking about the launch and his team.

He realized that the most critical three days of his life lay before him, yet he also had an incredible feeling of calm that somehow it would all work out. Somehow it would all come together. The feeling even surprised him, but after the last week and a half he was getting used to surprises. Life, he was learning, could change in a flash.

One minute you think you're headed toward certain destruction and the next you're sitting on a bus strategizing about business with a bunch of people who probably never actually had taken a business class in their lives. The biggest surprise of all is that what they say actually works. Yes, George was getting used to surprises.

Chapter 22

Better Today than Yesterday

What's missing? What can I do better? How can I show my team I'm on their bus? George thought as he sat at the bus stop Wednesday morning thinking about his conversations with Jamie and José and his team's overall performance yesterday. The day's events ran through his mind in the way a football coach would revisit every play of a game or a dancer would rehash every move, every twist, and every turn of her performance. It is then that one remembers successes and mistakes and thinks of "should haves" and "could haves." It is a critical time that one improves if they are willing to learn, grow from mistakes, and build upon their success. George had always known this but somewhere along the way he had forgotten to stop learning and growing.

But now he was thinking clearly again and he remembered the great advice he had received from his college lacrosse coach, who had told him, "The goal is not to be better than anyone else but rather be better than you were yesterday." Indeed George wanted to be a better leader, a better person, a better husband, and a better father. He wanted José to feel good about working for him and he wanted Jamie to see that he wasn't going to implode. George's goal was to improve every day, help his team improve, and hopefully deliver an incredible launch to the executives of the NRG Company. He knew it was a long shot but hope and a desire to change and succeed were all he had left. His team had made great strides yesterday but he also knew they would need a lot more to turn the impossible into the possible and succeed on Friday. He knew something was missing but he wasn't sure what.

He pulled the rock Joy had given him out of his pocket. Although he felt silly for carrying around a rock in his pocket, everything else Joy had said made sense so he figured she must have had a good reason for giving it to him. He looked at it and remembered what she had said, "When you find the value in the rock you will find the treasure in yourself and in others." Maybe there is a gem inside here or something like that, he thought. Then he laughed at the crazy thought. No way. As if Joy would give me a rock with a diamond inside it. I don't think so, he said to himself. But what value could possibly be found in this rock, he wondered. Maybe it was from an ancient civilization or something like that. Or maybe the rock symbolizes strength. It certainly did help me when I was having it out with Tom, he thought. Or maybe it was from a special river. Or perhaps the rock became valuable because it was a special gift from her and because she had received it as a special gift from her teacher. I have no idea, he thought. Maybe Joy will have some answers about the rock and also about what I'm missing as a leader, he thought as Bus #11 pulled up.

Chapter 23

Feeling Good

 George heard a loud chant as he approached the bus. "I feel great. Yes. I feel great. Yes. I feel great. Yes," echoed throughout the bus and through his ears as all the passengers were cheering and throwing their arms into the air. Joy, of course, was leading the chant before she stopped to greet George.

"Hey, Sugar, how are you feeling today?"

"Good," he said. "What's going on here? Why are you all cheering like this?"

"Emotions, George. They can lift you up or bring you down. We like to say that E-motion stands for energy in motion and your emotional state is all about how the energy is flowing through you. So instead of letting negative emotions take you down a dark road of negativity, sadness, and despair we can take control of our emotions, charge ourselves up, and let the positive energy flow."

"Makes sense but it seems a little corny," George said.

"Of course it does," she answered. "We know that. But the people on this bus are walking off happy, charged up, and ready for the day while many on the other buses are dreading another day at work. What would you rather be, corny and happy or buttoned up and miserable? It's an easy choice, don't you think?"

George couldn't argue with her. He had been miserable long enough to know he would rather look silly and be happy than miserable. Anything but miserable.

"The key is to feel good," she continued. "When you feel good everyone around you feels good. And we're not talking about feeling good from a double latte or candy bar kind of feeling good. We're talking about a feeling joy, happiness, enthusiasm, gratitude, passion, and excitement kind of feeling good. Remember, George, the gifts you bring to the world are not found in your resume, accomplishments, or presents to others. The gift is your presence of feeling good and being happy and bringing this to others. Being around happy and positive people makes people feel happy and positive. Too many people try to please others and this only makes them unhappy. Better to focus on feeling good and letting this feeling and happiness shine on others. When you feel good you give from power. When you feel bad and try to feel good by pleasing others you only give away your power . . . and this makes you weaker. Am I making sense?"

She was making perfect sense to George. He had spent his life trying to please his boss, his wife, and everyone else only to grow more unhappy every day. Now he was feeling good again. The Energy Vampires were off his bus and his team was on the right track. Feeling good definitely made a difference.

But George was also still thinking about his day yesterday and was still trying to figure out what was missing. He told Joy about his day and his meetings with Jamie and José and how they had blasted him with the truth and how it had really made him realize how destructive he had been as a leader. He told her about the positive team meetings and the way they all had responded. Then he asked her point blank what wasn't he doing that he could be doing that would make the difference. "After all, I'm feeling good and they are responding but not as much as I would like. There is still something missing. I know we can do even more. There has to be something more than just feeling good."

"There is more," Joy responded immediately. "You're definitely a changed man, George. I'm proud of you for that. But now you got to be a changed leader. And the key to this change is your heart. What's missing is your heart. This is what we've got to help you tap and share with others. It's all about heart, Georgey. I hope you are ready because once you take the next step on your journey there ain't no turning back."

Chapter 24

Lead with Heart

 George wondered what Joy meant when she said he had no heart. "What do you mean I have no heart?" George questioned as he pointed to himself. "It's right here. It's not missing."

"Come on, George. I know you got one. But your heart has been cold, negative, and numb for so long it has gotten closed off. And it doesn't open completely overnight. All this stuff you've been dealing with lately has been opening your heart which is a good thing. I once heard this saying that God keeps breaking your heart until it opens. And ain't that the truth. Think about it. Every struggle, every challenge, every adversity brings you closer to your heart, to your true self, to who you really are. Sometimes you got to be broken down to the point where you feel powerless to discover your ultimate and true power. And I see this with you. That's why you came on my bus. Because it was time to get in touch with the real, positive, and powerful you."

George thought about his flat tire, his marriage problems, his work crisis, and his meetings with José and Jamie, and he knew she was right. Everything was causing him to stop blaming others and start looking at himself. He had never thought about having an open or closed heart before, though. He was just glad he hadn't had a heart attack yet.

"And now it's time for you to lead, George," she declared. "Not manage. I'm talking leading with positive contagious leadership. This is what your team craves. They want you to lead with heart. It's the missing piece you have been asking about. The heart is your power center. It's where contagious positive leadership comes from and the more open, powerful, and positive it is the more powerful you are."

"She's not kidding," Marty spoke up from the back of the bus. "This is not rah rah motivational stuff. It's real peak performance science now. In fact I found research published in numerous scientific journals conducted by the Institute of HeartMath, heartmath.org." Marty picked up his computer and showed George. The screen looked like this.

- The heart acts as an emotional conductor and radiates how you are feeling to every cell in the body via the heart's electromagnetic field; this energy field can be detected up to 5 to 10 feet away.

- The heart's electromagnetic field is 5,000 times more powerful than the brain.

"Ten feet away, 5,000 times more powerful than the brain!" Joy shouted as she zeroed in on George to make sure he understood the significance of this research. "It means that we are broadcasting our positive or negative energy every moment of the day via our heart and people are picking up and receiving this signal."

"That's how we can tell if people are being real or fake," Janice said, joining the conversation. "We can feel their heart and know if it is sincere or just a facade."

"You know it," Joy said. "And it's why we have expressions like *He has a big heart* or *She puts her heart into her work* or *They have a lot of heart*. We're all walking around broadcasting our feelings energetically and whether it's positive, negative, excited, calm, angry, or nervous, everyone feels it. Like I told you the other day, George, it's all energy. Your employees are tuning into your broadcast station and they want your energy. They need you more now than ever. And you need them. If you want them to receive more positive and powerful energy, then you got to broadcast that power by opening and tapping the power of your heart."

"But I don't know how to do this," George said as he looked around anxiously at Marty and Joy knowing he had only two more days before his product launch. "How do I lead with heart?"

Chapter 25

Chief Energy Officer

 The answer would come not from Joy but from someone else on the bus. Someone who had hardly spoken but who had a lot of experience with being a positive, contagious leader. His name was Jack and he was a middle-aged man with a bald head and one of those big white sparkling smiles that made you smile. When he spoke everyone listened and now was his time to tell George what he knew.

"It's time for you to become the CEO of the NRG Company," Jack commanded with the confidence of a seasoned leader as he fixed his tie and brushed off his suit jacket.

George thought this guy had completely lost his mind. "Sir, I'm just a manager. Not even an executive. I've got two days. Please tell me how I'm going to be the CEO of my company and what it has to do with leading from the heart."

"First, call me Jack. Second, CEO doesn't stand for chief executive officer anymore. It stands for Chief Energy Officer. Why energy? Because energy is the currency of personal and professional success today. If you don't have it you can't lead, inspire, or make a difference. And the great thing about being a Chief Energy Officer is that anyone in your company including you can become one. Deciding to become a Chief Energy Officer means that you share positive, powerful, and contagious energy with your co-workers, employees, and customers! It means you communicate from the heart," Jack said as he put his hand on his chest. "Now, George, I'm sure you heard that the big buzzword in business today is *emotional intelligence.*" George nodded as Marty yelled from the back, "Research says it's responsible for 80 percent of adult success."

"Yes, it is, Marty," Jack added, "and what emotional intelligence (EI) really is all about is tapping the power of your heart when you are leading, selling, and communicating. EI and heartfelt leadership are one and the same. It's all about communicating effectively and contagiously with others. And you know what this means when you really simplify it? It means that people like you respect you and they want to follow you. Now I'm not saying you can become a Chief Energy Officer overnight but if you are going to lead your team to victory on Friday, you have to start now."

Then quietly he asked, "Can I tell you a little story?"

"Of course," answered George.

"Before your eyes, you see me, a confident leader. I

know who I am. I know what I am here to do and I know how to lead. Not only am I the chief executive officer of my company but I am indeed one of the Chief Energy Officers as well. But several years ago this was not the case. Several years ago, just like you, I was on this bus and Joy, dear Joy, truly an angel sent from heaven, saved my job, my company, and my life. Do you want to know how?" George nodded as his eyes were fixed on this confident leader.

"I was running a major division in my company. They had handpicked me out of business school years before and many of the higher ups called me the Chosen One. I had all the knowledge in the world. I had the resume, the pedigree, and the work ethic. Man, I worked hard. For 25 years I walked, no, I ran up the corporate ladder of success.

"But looking back, what I see I didn't have was heart. I wasn't a real leader. I kicked people off my bus all the time without thinking about it and I led by fear, and fear doesn't last. It had worked early in my career but over time we had a severe retention and morale problem in my division and productivity had dropped significantly. Performance plunged. Negativity grew and sales dropped so low we almost caused the company to go into bankruptcy. The board wanted to fire me but one guy, my mentor, who was the president of the company, believed in me and said he would give me a chance to turn the situation around. But I didn't have any hope. I had failed and decided to give up and I mean give all of it up. But wouldn't you believe on the one day I had decided to leave early to give up not just my job but my life, I met Joy."

George just sat there in shock, saying no under his breath.

"Yes, George, I was going to give it all up. The pain was too big, the failure too large. The expectation I had never lived up to. I know what you are thinking. Looking back it's hard to believe. I can't even believe that had been my thought process back then but I was down, real down, until Joy lifted me up. Her smile made my day. Her words energized me. She woke me up.

"So I decided not to give up and started taking her bus to work. You know, I drive 20 extra minutes just to get to the bus stop on her route. I became a Chief Energy Officer because of her and now I have developed a thriving company filled with Chief Energy Officers who use her 10 rules to create success and positive energy every day. She saved my life and job so now I want to help you, George. That's how positive energy works. A life touches a life that touches a life. It spreads, one person at a time. And to help you spread positive energy to your team and the world you need to know rule #7, which answers your question about how to lead with heart."

With happy tears in her eyes, Joy directed Danny to show George rule #7. Here's what it said.

Rule #7

Enthusiasm Attracts More Passengers and Energizes Them During the Ride.

Joy wanted to speak but she was still choked up. No matter how many times she had heard Jack tell that story it still brought tears to her eyes. She remembered the day they had met. In fact she remembered every meaningful conversation she had ever had on her bus. And as she looked at George she saw another great opportunity to help change the life of someone who had so much to give but just needed to learn how to give it. She wanted him to succeed as much as he did and knew he was in good company with a man who had not only learned her principles but who lived them and shared them every day at his company.

Jack looked at the sign Danny held up and looked at George. Their eyes met and Jack continued sharing his energy and knowledge with a guy who needed him more now than ever. "Chief Energy Officers live and work with enthusiasm, George. They tap the power of their heart by getting excited about being alive, by filling up with loads of positive energy, and by being optimistic about life and work. They don't let fear stop them. No, they charge forward with positive and powerful energy and look at challenges like the one you are facing on Friday as an opportunity to learn, grow, and succeed."

Marty yelled once again from the back of the bus. "*Enthusiasm* comes from the Greek word *entheos*, which means 'inspired' or 'filled with the divine.'"

"Indeed it does," Jack confirmed, "and I'm here to tell you, George, that when you get excited and enthusiastic about your life and work you bring this powerful divine energy to everything you do, and people notice. They can see it and feel it. When you're enthusiastic, people want to get on your bus. Your bus is energized and people say, 'Hey, I want to get on that bus.' Employees from different departments want to help you out. You get a reputation as someone people want to work for. Customers want to work with you. Salespeople come to you for advice because they're looking for that enthusiastic energy to increase their sales. When you live and work with enthusiasm, people are drawn to you like moths to a light. Walt Whitman said that we convince by our presence, and when you are enthusiastic you project an energy that convinces people to get on and stay on your bus. It's powerful energy, George. Joy taught me this and it works."

Jack was convincing but he didn't need to convince George that it worked. As Jack spoke, George remembered how enthusiasm had helped him get his first job. They had told him they loved his fire. He thought about how enthusiasm in trying to get a date with his wife eventually influenced her to give him a shot. He reflected on how enthusiastic he had been during his early years at the NRG Company and wondered what had happened. Where along the way had he lost his spark? But that was the past, he thought. Now he just wanted to feel that fire burn inside him again. He wanted to be everything Jack was describing, and as he was listening he was thinking about how to bring that energy to work today.

Jack continued his teachings. "Remember what Joy also said. 'When you feel good, others around you feel good.' Well, when you are enthusiastic you feel real good and this makes the people around you feel real good. I once had one customer tell me that he had bought from my sales guy not necessarily because they loved our product but because they loved his energy. They were excited because he was excited. They were excited about being on his bus.

"I don't care what product you are selling, what division or team you are leading, or what product launch you are presenting. People are always buying you and your energy. The simple truth is that when you are excited people get excited about where your bus is going and this makes them want to get on and stay on your bus.

Joy had been quiet for some time and although she admired how her protégé had become a master of teaching her principles she wanted to make sure George knew something that Jack hadn't mentioned so she joined the conversation. "But this doesn't mean you're all fake and annoying either, George. Enthusiasm doesn't mean you bounce off the walls all hyper and all. The kind of enthusiasm Jack and I talk about is real. You don't have to force it or push it. You just live it. You let your presence do the convincing. So just focus on getting excited and enthusiastic yourself and let your energy do the talking. Focus today on becoming the heart of your team. Realize that just as every cell in the body beats to the frequency of the heart, everyone around you will beat to your frequency and your energy. Just as the heart radiates energy to every cell you must radiate positive energy and enthusiasm to every member of your team. Most of all teach this to your team. Let them know they, too, can become a Chief Energy Officer. Let them know that anyone can become the heart of their organization because no matter where you are and what you do, when you live and work with enthusiasm people around you will beat to your frequency.

"Is that why my team was in such disarray?" George asked looking at Joy and Jack. "Because I was broadcasting a negative signal and negative energy on a daily basis?"

"Well, honestly yes," Jack answered. "Negative people often tend to create negative cultures whereas positive corporate cultures are created by positive people. The energy of a company or team is cultivated by the energy and enthusiasm of the leaders and each person in the organization who contributes to the collective energy and culture of it. In turn this collective energy influences each person's energy in the organization creating a perpetual cycle of positive energy or negative energy. So when people ask me what my company's most important asset is I tell them it is energy. Not gas or oil, I say but the people and the energy they bring to their work. And this positive energy is what makes us successful."

"The numbers don't lie," Marty said always looking to add research to the discussion. "Daniel Goleman, author of *Emotional Intelligence* (Bloomsbury, 1996; Bantam, 1997), explains that a positive company with a positive corporate culture will outperform their negative counterparts every time. It's also important to note that if you would invest in the companies voted the best places to work, where people are full of positive energy and enthusiasm, you would significantly outperform the stock market averages. So it appears that a positive culture is also good for revenue and the bottom line."

"You hear that?" Joy said. "It's all about energy, George. What's been missing is enthusiasm. The most successful teams have it; every team wants it but very few have it. And it starts with you. When you have it, they'll have it. When you get energized, they'll get energized. So it's time to take your energy meter to the next level. Are you ready, George?"

"*Yes* I am!" He was fired up and ready to take action. The bus was a few miles away from his office but he felt like jumping off and running the rest of the way. Yet he knew that would only tire him out and he needed all the energy he could muster right now. So he decided to stay on the bus and listen to what else Joy would have to say. This was a good thing because the next rule he would learn would completely change everything.

Chapter 26

Love Your Passengers

As Joy motored down the road she thought about what to say next. She looked away from the road and out to the far right. High above the road was one of those signs that said LOVE IS THE ANSWER.—GOD. She pointed at the sign and directed George and her passengers to look. "Isn't it amazing," she said, "how the signs of life always appear at the right time to guide us on our journey? I mean if you are open to the signs and look for them they will always tell you where your bus needs to go and what you need for your ride. And best of all when you use the signs to find the right path and make a decision to follow it, God will move heaven and earth to support you. The right people show up. The right situations fall into place. Obstacles dissolve. Creative ideas appear. It's how it all works. I don't make the rules. I just understand and teach them." Then she looked at George and said, "That sign was meant for you, Sugar, and if you have any doubt throw it out because Danny's going to show you rule #8." Danny lifted up the sign, which said this.

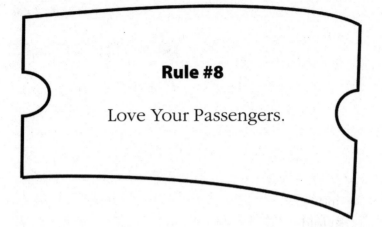

Rule #8

Love Your Passengers.

"Don't ignore the signs, George. Love is the answer for the team's success," she said as George was looking a little surprised right now. He had never heard of anyone talking about love and business in the same sentence.

"Enthusiasm is important. But love is the answer. To really, really, and I mean really, tap the power of your heart and lead with positive, contagious energy you must love your passengers. You've got to become a Love Magnet," she said.

At once everyone on the bus cheered in unison, "LOOOOVVVVE Magnet!"

"What the heck is a Love Magnet?" George asked looking around, not sure if he even wanted to know the answer.

"Well, you don't become a Love Magnet by wearing expensive cologne or perfume," she said. "You don't become one by walking around sharing cheesy lines at bars."

Good, George thought, because he didn't wear cologne or go to bars.

"You become a Love Magnet by loving your employees, your customers, your company, and your family. You become a Love Magnet by "sharing the love generously.""

Jack stepped in and said, "I know it sounds corny to talk about love in the business world, George, but she's right. All any of us really want is to be loved, and all your employees really want is your love." George thought of José and realized they were onto something.

He told them about José and how all he wanted was to be recognized and cared about. George had promised he would do something for José to show him but didn't know what.

"Love is all he wants, George. You can give all the trophies and awards you want, and sure a raise would be a good idea for him, but eventually the gift is forgotten and the excitement of the raise wears off and what remains is an emotional feeling, a feeling of whether you love them. That's what it's all about, George. José and your team want to know that you care about them. They want to know that you are concerned about their future and welfare. They need to know that you love them. It can't be just about you and your job. It also has to be about them. And when you love them, they'll love you back. If you treat them like a number or your next promotion or your next bonus, they'll treat you like a number. But if you really love and care about them they will love you back by working hard for you, by being loyal to you, by surprising

115

Love Your Passengers

you with amazing initiative and success stories, and by teaching you as much as you will teach them. It's the same with sales, George. The best salespeople are Love Magnets. When customers know you love them instead of just seeing them as a new car or boat, they'll never leave you. When they feel the love they will send you more business and refer more people to you. People do business with people they like and who love them. The more love you put out the more that comes back to you. And when your team knows you love them and feel the love from you they will want to stay on your bus wherever it goes. So enthusiasm gets them excited about being on your bus, but love is what keeps them on the bus."

"This all sounds wonderful," George said skeptically. "It really does. But talking about love and business is one thing and practicing it is another. Let's face it, the last time I checked, giving hugs at work is not too popular with Human Resources. Love in theory is wonderful but how do you practice it at work is my question. And how do you also get past all the people who think love is weak and for wimps?"

"Great point," Jack said. "It's not easy. No one said love was, especially in business. But with commitment and practice there is no better way to enhance the performance and productivity of your team. Regarding love being for the weak, well, they just don't understand the research. Tell them, Marty."

Marty explained how a human being is stronger when they are thinking positive, loving thoughts than when they are thinking negative, angry thoughts. "People think love is a weak emotion," he said, "but really it's the strongest most powerful emotion available to us. Just try to bench press a lot of weight. If you are thinking loving, positive thoughts you'll be stronger than if you are thinking negative, angry thoughts."

"The good news," Jack continued, "is we have the perfect resource to put love into action. We spent a lot of time and energy on this and came up with five ways to love your passengers, and these ways are the best practices I have implemented in my company, with amazing results," Jack said as he handed George a sheet of paper featuring the five strategies.

George scanned the sheet of paper but quickly looked out the window and noticed they were about to arrive at his office. "Well, we obviously don't have time to go over these but is there any one of these strategies I should start immediately?" George asked, wanting to do all he could as soon as he could.

"Well, more than anything, George, love takes time," Joy said. "It's a process not a goal. Love is something that needs to be nurtured. But if there is one thing I urge you to start immediately it's focus on bringing out the best in each person on your team. When you love someone you want the best for them. You want them to shine. And the best way to do this is to help them discover the value inside them."

"Like the rooooooooock," George said slowly nodding his head.

"Yes, like the rock, George. I was waiting for you to ask me about the rock. You still have it?" she asked.

"Yes, I do. Right here," George said as he held it up to show her.

"Good because if you lost it I would have to put a hurt'n on you," she said, laughing out loud.

Joy then took a towel, poured water onto it, and handed it to George. "Now, take this wet towel here and wipe the rock, George. Wipe it good." George scrubbed and scrubbed and scrubbed and to his surprise the black came off the rock and what was left was nothing but shiny gold.

"Is this what I think it is?" he asked.

"You bet it is, my brother," Joy answered as she jokingly grabbed the rock out of George's hand. "That's why you're one lucky man that you didn't lose it." George closed his eyes and laughed.

"You see, George, dust on gold doesn't change the nature of gold. It's still gold. And your team members just like you have a lot of dust on them. The key is to realize that inside every one of them is gold that wants to shine. The value is on the inside. Help them find their gold, George, as I have helped you. Remove their dust. Help them discover their strengths. Allow them to do what they do best. Let them utilize their strengths on a daily basis and know that as they utilize their strengths, their value and the value of the team will increase tenfold. That's love. Letting people share their gifts and strengths is real love. And by you loving them and by you helping them find their gold they will shine and so will you. That's what being a Chief Energy Officer is all about; when you bring out the best in others you can't help bringing out the best in yourself."

At that moment Joy stopped talking, Jack stopped talking, and the bus was completely silent. All the passengers knew what this meant. George was ready.

Joy had a proud look on her face. They had shared with George what he needed to know and she felt he was ready to make some amazing progress the next two days before his big presentation. But she also knew that this was about much more than just a product launch. Sure, she wanted him to enjoy success but she also knew that whether his product launch was successful was really irrelevant in the grand scheme of things. He wouldn't see it that way, of course, so if the launch was a disaster she would prepare to explain once again that everything happens for a reason and no matter what he did or where he went from this point on he was now equipped with the rules to create an incredible life and career at the NRG Company or somewhere else. He had the rules and with rules came incredible power. His big meeting this Friday would be just one leg of a long journey and to truly enjoy the ride of his life he would need to know the final two rules. Without them, he would be missing out on the ultimate fuel for a meaningful and powerful life. No time for that today, Joy thought, as they pulled up to George's office building. Tomorrow we'll get into that.

As George walked off the bus, Joy shouted, "Give it

all you got today, George! Remember enthusiasm, love, and gold. And don't forget to love that wife of yours. She needs it, too. Share all the love you got and tomorrow we'll be here to recharge you!"

George put his hand over his heart and then over his mouth and blew a kiss to Joy and the Energy Bus passengers. They didn't know it but he was more thankful than any of them could possibly realize. As he turned his back and walked away from the bus, ready to share the love and energy, Joy turned to Jack and he looked at her.

"He's ready,"she said.

"I agree," confirmed Jack.

Chapter 27

Love Rules

 As George walked toward his building he glanced at the sheet of paper Jack had given him that featured the five ways to love your passengers. The rules intrigued him so much that he stopped at the bench just outside the door, sat down, and began reading intently. If I've got the love to give, I need to start giving it today, he thought. So I better learn all I can right now. Here's what George read. (Turn the page.)

FIVE WAYS TO LOVE YOUR PASSENGERS

1. *Make Time for Them*—When you love someone or something, you spend time with them. You nurture your relationship with them. You can't nurture business relationships sitting at your desk, just as you can't spend quality time with your spouse if you are watching television. So the key is to come out of your office and get to know your team. Spend time with them. Meet with them individually. Get to know them as people, not numbers. Just as you would tend to a garden, you need to cultivate your team with love. And while you are with them it is important to be present with them. Be engaged in the present moment. Don't be thinking about 10 things you have to do that day or the 10 other people you need to meet with. Really be with that person and focus your energy on them. They will feel the difference.

2. *Listen to Them*—One of the most important factors that determines a high management approval rating is whether the manager listens to the employee. Does the manager hear what the employee has to say? Does the manager listen to the ideas and needs of the employee? Your employees and customers just want to be heard, so listen to them and hear them. We're not talking about some active listening class technique, either. We're talking about really sitting down and listening with your heart and caring about what they have today. Empathy is the key. When employees feel seen and heard, there is a moistening in the eyes. Yet researchers estimate that in more than 95 percent of daily interactions there is no moistening in the eyes, according to *High Energy Living*, by Robert K. Cooper (New American Library, 2002). For instance when you ask someone how they are doing, an easy way to show you are listening is to actually wait for the answer and make eye contact.

3. *Recognize Them*—We don't mean trophies or some awards dinner. We want you to make it real personal. Honor them for who they are and what they do. Recognize them as a person as much as a business professional. One leader we know sends each employee a personal birthday card with a handwritten note, not some electronic fake signature but a real note. While it's not possible to do this in every company, every manager can do this with their team. Another company allows employees to choose the UPC codes for their new products. Employees choose codes that feature their birth dates, anniversaries, kids' birthdays, and so on. This makes it very personal. Another very powerful way to recognize them is to praise them when they are doing things right.

(Continued)

FIVE WAYS TO LOVE YOUR PASSENGERS
(Continued)

The more you recognize them for doing things right the more they will do things right. Feed the positive dog inside them and watch it grow.

4. *Serve Them*—A great leader once said, the higher you get in an organization the more it is your duty to serve the people below you rather than having the people below serve you. The key is to serve their growth, their future, their career, and their spirits so they enjoy work, life, and being on your bus. The more you serve their growth the more they will help you grow.

5. *Bring Out the Best in Them*—We saved this one for last because it's the most important. When you love someone you want the best for them. You want them to be successful and happy. You want to bring out the best in them. Thus the best way any leader can demonstrate their love for their team is to help each person discover their strengths and provide an opportunity for that person to utilize them. When you create a system that provides a way for your people to shine you not only bring out the best in them but in the rest of the team and company as well. If you really want to love your team, help them do what they do best. It's that simple.

Chapter 28

Fear and Trust

 George walked into his office building like he owned it, ready to love and inspire his team. But as he walked toward the elevator and thought about the mountainous challenge that lay in front of him, self-doubt reared its ugly head again as it always had. What if they don't love me back, he thought. It wouldn't be the first time love had gone unanswered. What if I can't inspire my team? What if I can't inspire myself? What if it's all too late? Fear consumed him and he felt like someone had hauled off and punched him right in the stomach. Doubled over and unable to breathe, he looked out the window and saw his bus driving away. He knew that what Joy and Jack had told him were powerful truths, but living them and making them real was an entirely different matter altogether. Caught between knowledge and action, George was paralyzed by fear.

The elevator door opened and closed as he just stood there unable to move. On the bus he had felt safe but now he felt like a chained gladiator about to be thrown into a cage with a bunch of lions that didn't care about the bus rules. His mind was so preoccupied with his negative thoughts that he didn't notice a familiar rival standing in front of him, nervous and shaking.

Michael spoke first. "I know I quit, George, and I know I told you that your bus is going to crash but I've been doing a lot of thinking, and Jamie called to say that your bus is cruising now. She said the team has been talking and it's like you are a changed man and they're all excited. I'm here to ask for another chance, George. I know I can help the team and I know I can help you." George, who was trying to catch his breath, stood up straight. Would it be a big mistake to give Michael another chance? He might still be an Energy Vampire, yet they really could use him now. George remembered reading an article about Richard Branson, who gave one of his employees a second chance and the guy went on to become one of his most trusted leaders over the years. George's fear was dissipating, he was thinking more clearly now. "Okay, you got it. I'll give you another shot, but I need you to be a Chief Energy Officer."

"Chief energy what?" Michael asked.

"I'll explain upstairs. Just get ready for an incredible day."

The elevator opened and Michael walked in. "You coming, George?"

"I'll be upstairs in a minute."

"Thank you for everything," Michael said with a sincere and humble look. "I won't let you down." As the elevator started to close George responded, "It's good to have you back."

George looked outside at the spot where the Energy Bus had dropped him off. He thought about what had just happened. Joy had just talked about looking for signs and letting them guide you on your path, and he couldn't help but wonder if Michael was a sign.

Maybe Michael's asking for another chance meant that George's team was ready to follow him, and maybe his giving Michael another chance meant George was ready to lead and love his team. Michael was an obstacle but maybe this meant that the obstacles were dissolving. Joy had talked about being on the right path and perhaps he was on it, everything lining up to clear the way for his bus. After all, as in a movie or a dream, Michael had approached at just the right moment to wake George up and help him move past his fear. This "vampire" had asked to come back just when they needed him most.

This made George think of the dream he had had the other night and it all became clear. The dream had been a sign, too, letting him know to trust. He was the driver of his bus and he had a choice. The decision to keep Michael and trust him was a choice and so was the decision to move forward with trust or stay paralyzed by fear. Sure, he was racing toward possible destruction of his career, and his bus could surely crash but he had a choice to believe it was all going to work out or quit now. Jack had told him that Chief Energy Officers overcome challenges by charging forward with trust and optimism, and that's what George was determined to do. Through trust he knew he would tap into the ultimate GPS system (God's Positioning System) and it would continue to guide him just as it had been guiding him all along. He couldn't ignore the signs. They were all pointing in the right direction and the lights were all green telling him to go. I'm not going to live with fear and let fear get in my way, he thought. After all, they don't call it "a leap of fear." They call it "a leap of faith" for a reason. If I can trust in God, in myself, and in my team, then they can trust in each other and in me, he said to himself, as the fear he had felt earlier had turned into faith and faith had turned into resolve. George then stepped into the elevator, and now he was truly ready to take the leap of his life.

Chapter 29

The Next Day

George huffed and puffed as he sprinted the last few blocks to the bus stop. He couldn't believe he hadn't heard his alarm go off. He had stayed at the office till 3 A.M. with José and Michael trying to get caught up, so he hadn't gotten much sleep. It was Thursday and with one day before the biggest presentation of his life he needed to talk with Joy and Jack more now than ever. As the bus was pulling away from the stop George ran up alongside it and banged on the window trying to get someone's attention, anyone's attention, but no one heard him and the bus took off.

George went back to the bench and sat down feeling tired and dejected. Now, he wouldn't get to tell them about his incredible day yesterday and how his team had responded unbelievably to his enthusiasm. He wanted to tell them about how he had held a team meeting and had talked about what it meant to be a Chief Energy Officer.

He had met with José and had told him he was giving him a raise if he didn't get fired, and more importantly

George had told him that no matter what, he would always be there as a mentor and resource for José. He shared the love with all his team and he could tell they felt it. The team was energized, the ideas were flowing, and they had accomplished more in one day than they had all month.

George's only concern was that more people hadn't worked late with him. Tonight they would need to pull another late night to get the presentation (the graphics, the sound effects, and the overall flow) perfected, and he would need more than two members of his team to work late. He needed to ask Joy and Jack their advice about what to do, and now he had missed this important opportunity. I'll just wait for the next bus and use this time to think of a solution, he thought, trying to stay positive about the situation. He was becoming a believer and was learning not to let little setbacks crush his spirit. Trust, he kept saying to himself as he focused on his breathing the way Joy had taught him last week.

When George arrived at his office he was surprised to find a letter sitting on his chair. It had been written on computer paper and when he opened it up he couldn't help but smile. It was from Joy. It said:

Now George, don't think I wrote this and drove the bus at the same time. I'm not that good. Janice wrote it for me when we realized you weren't going to be on the bus today. Jack figured you probably stayed at work really late to get prepared for the presentation and got a late start this morning. We had a hunch that you would need to know rule #9 more now than ever so Marty ran this letter up to your office. Here it is.

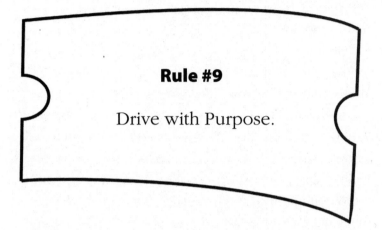

Rule #9

Drive with Purpose.

Purpose is the ultimate fuel for our journey through life, George. When we drive with purpose we don't get tired or bored and our engines don't burn out. I know you are probably pumped up for this product launch and you should be but you have to ask yourself what's going to energize you after the launch. Every job on the planet, even that of a professional athlete or movie star, can get old and mundane if we let it. Purpose keeps it fresh. Let me give you an example.

There's a story about when President Lyndon Johnson visited NASA and as he was walking the halls he came across a janitor who was cleaning up a storm, like the Energizer bunny with a mop in his hand.

The president walked over to the janitor and told him he was the best janitor he had ever seen and the janitor replied, "Sir, I'm not just a janitor, I helped put a man on the moon." See George, even though he was cleaning floors he had a bigger purpose and vision for his life. This is what kept him going and helped him excel in his job. People call me a bus driver. But I see my purpose as much more than that. I'm an Energy Ambassador and coach helping people transform their energy and lives. Sure, driving a bus gets old; every job does. But knowing I've saved lives and wondering whose life I'm going to touch today, now that keeps me going and the energy flowing. That's why my passengers stay on my bus, because I'm driving with purpose. When you fuel up with purpose you find the excitement in the mundane, the passion in the everyday, and the extraordinary in the ordinary. Purpose is what life is all about. Everyone's out there trying to find their purpose when all you have to do is find the bigger purpose in the here and now and your purpose will find you.

There's no spirit in companies anymore because there's no spirit in the people who work for these companies. Unfortunately too many companies have been far too successful at creating a culture and system that zaps people's energy and spirit. And Jack says, then they wonder why they have morale, retention, negativity, and performance issues. Don't be one of these leaders who get inspired only when there's a big project or deadline or job at stake. It won't last and it won't lead to greatness. Foster spirit and allow it to move through your team by fueling up with purpose. Find the bigger purpose and vision before your product launch and let it fuel you and your team every day thereafter. I can't tell you what this purpose and vision are. Only you can decide this.

Remember you're driving the bus. You have the best view and vision so you'll also need to communicate your vision and purpose with your passengers. Once you find your bigger purpose and vision then share it with your team. Once they are a part of this bigger purpose and vision they will work harder and longer for you.

Jack told me to tell you that he spent too many long nights by himself before big presentations until he learned this rule. So drive with purpose today and every day and cultivate it in your team and they'll not only stay on your bus when it's cruising but they'll also get out to help push it when it breaks down. Shared purpose keeps a team energized and together. Share it, George.

JOY

George couldn't help but smile and shake his head. Less than two weeks ago he had had a flat tire and couldn't catch a break. Now after missing the bus he still received rule #9 and Joy and Jack had provided him with exactly the answers he sought, as if knowing the questions he was going to ask. The only question he still needed to answer was what his bigger purpose and vision were. It's hard to get excited about lightbulbs, he thought, as he looked at Joy's letter and realized that there was still one sheet he hadn't read yet. He placed it on top of the other pages and chuckled once he realized it was from Marty.

> Hi, George. Marty here. There was a study conducted where two airplane design teams were separated. One team saw a model of the finished product and was given a vision that they were building the fastest, newest, most advanced airplane ever built. The other team were separated into small groups who were told to design each piece without knowing what the end design and vision would be. Not surprisingly the team who had a vision for what they were building worked twice as long and hard and finished in half the time as the other group. Thought you should know this.
>
> MARTY

This gave George an idea and it was so good that if Marty was in front of him George would hug him. Well, maybe not hug him but definitely give him a high five. George called his team into the conference room for a meeting where he was going to share his ideas with them. His team was on his bus. Now he wanted them to propel the bus forward with purpose, vision, and inspiration. He just hoped his ideas would work.

Chapter 30

The Team Gets Inspired

 Instead of telling the team his bigger purpose and vision, George had an idea to let his team formulate a shared purpose and vision together. Rather than being told what their purpose and vision should be, he thought it would be more powerful, meaningful, and inspiring if the team formulated what they wanted it to be. And powerful it was. George explained the several examples Joy had shared with him and immediately the team ran with it. They started sharing ideas back and forth. Like a game of ping pong the energy was bouncing around the room while Jamie wrote all their ideas on a white board.

Then over the course of an hour and many discussions later they narrowed it down to three central principles that everyone, including George, agreed on. For today and every day hereafter they would not just be a team who brought new lightbulbs to market but rather a team that:

1. Strived for greatness and produced great ideas, great marketing campaigns, and great results.

2. Worked with purpose and spirit to develop Chief Energy Officers not only within their team but within their entire company by sharing the positive energy.

3. Shared the light. No longer would they be people who just made lightbulbs. Instead they would see themselves as people whose lightbulbs helped a child read in bed before bedtime, an elderly person find their medicine at night, a working parent wake up early for work, or a college student study for an important exam. Their work would light up the rooms and the lives of every man, woman, and child who ever turned on a light switch and benefited from the light of their bulb.

George noticed that the energy in the room was transformed. In the beginning of the meeting they had all seemed excited but now something was very different. Instead of each person trying to shine above the others they were all working together, contributing to the collective whole. Gone were the egos and personal agendas. The infighting had disappeared. They were fueling up with purpose and vision and were now contributing to something bigger than themselves. Like a successful rock band where each member plays a different instrument that magically contributes to an incredible sound, each member of his team was playing their parts, and the music was perfect. They were energized, synchronized, and fast becoming a team. They were on George's bus together with a shared vision, shared purpose, and collective powerful force of positive energy all focused in the same direction.

That night as George looked around the office at 2 A.M. he knew his idea had worked. He knew Joy and Jack had been right. He didn't have to work the late nights alone anymore. The team weren't just riding on his bus. They were pushing it from behind as well. George had a big smile on his face when he realized that every member of his team had stayed late with him to get ready for the product launch. Yes, they were on his bus and they were an energized, purpose-driven team. This was a good thing because tomorrow was game day and it would be the biggest triumph or most painful defeat of their professional lives.

The Team Gets Inspired

Chapter 31

Game Day

 It was Friday. Game day. Less than two weeks ago George had thought this day would be the end of his career at the NRG Company. Now he hoped it was a new beginning and a new opportunity that would allow him to share all the principles he had learned on the Energy Bus. He should have been tired but he wasn't. His wife had given him a big kiss as he left the house and he felt good knowing that no matter what happened at work their marriage was back on track. The kids were responding really well to his love and positive reinforcement and even the dog was enjoying being pet more. They might be poor if he lost his job but at least they would all be together. He had been thrilled when his wife had asked him the other night what he had done with the grumpy old George and he had given her a big hug when she said, "It feels like I'm meeting the man I fell in love with all over again. I don't know where you have been but I'm glad you are back."

I am back, he thought, as he sat on his usual bench

waiting for Joy's bus and I certainly don't ever want to go back to the places I've been. He couldn't imagine that happening, though. Joy had infected him with the positive energy bug and he would do whatever it took to keep that energy flowing.

George looked at his watch and noticed the bus was a little late. He was looking forward to seeing Joy, Jack, Marty, and the other passengers one last time. His car would be ready today after work and if by chance he still had his job, he would drive from now on to save time and bus fare. He hadn't thought of it before but it suddenly occurred to him that today would be his last day on the Energy Bus. As he thought about how much he would miss everyone, even Marty, Joy's bus arrived and stopped to pick him up one last time.

When the doors opened a man walked out repeating to himself, but loud enough for others to overhear, "Too blessed to be stressed." The man turned around and shouted, "Thanks, Joy!"

"Don't forget, too blessed to be stressed!" Joy shouted back.

Another energy convert, George thought, as he smiled and walked on the bus only to be greeted by loud applause from all the passengers.

"We all know today's the day, George, and we just want you to know we're behind you and sending positive energy your way today," Joy said.

George thanked her, Jack, and Marty for the letter and he thanked all the energy bus passengers for their support over the past two weeks. He told them about the team's incredible day and night at work yesterday and how rule #9 had made all the difference. "Thank you for being my energy team!" he shouted to everyone.

"So how you feeling today, Sugar?" Joy asked in a motherly tone.

"I'm feeling good. The team is ready. I'm ready. Nervous of course but who wouldn't be?"

"That's right, George. Who wouldn't be nervous? It's a sign of fear. We all have fear but the key to success is that your trust is bigger than your fear. A little fear is good but it is weak energy. It runs out. Trust is the high octane fuel that will take your bus wherever it needs to go."

"I like that," George said knowing that trust was a theme that had kept coming up in his life.

"It's like I was telling the gentleman who just got off the bus. All of us focus so much on what stresses us that we forget all the things we got to be thankful for. So when you head into that meeting today don't be stressed. Instead feel blessed. Be thankful you had this job all these years while so many are unemployed. Be thankful you have a supportive team and a family. Even be thankful that you can walk and talk. If you really started counting your blessings you would realize that they are greater than the stars in the sky. When you feel blessed you don't have time to be stressed. And this feeling of gratitude will fuel your performance today. It will lift you up and carry you over the finish line."

George looked around the bus and noticed that

everyone was intently listening to Joy, soaking up every word. They loved her as much as he did. He noticed an elderly gentleman sitting in the middle of the bus whom he hadn't seen before. The man was thin and wore a hat and glasses. He had one of those wrinkled faces you find in elderly people that could tell you about the places they have been, the things they have seen, the lives they have lived, and the lessons they have learned if you would only take the time to listen to them. The man had a sparkle in his eye that lit up when he made eye contact with George. George acknowledged him and the man lifted his hat and nodded with a greeting in return.

Yup, Joy thought, as she watched the interaction in her rearview mirror. The right people certainly come on our bus at the right time just when we need them.

"I'd like you to meet Eddy," she said directing George to the elderly gentleman. "Eddy and I met at the home where my father lives. Eddy's wife also had Alzheimer's and we met at the facility. Unfortunately Eddy's wife passed on and he had a real rough time with it. But after a year of mourning he's now living his life again and I'd say he has more energy and is busier than most twenty-year-olds I know. Tell him how old you are, Eddy."

"Eighty-eight," he replied.

"That's right, George, eighty-eight and he plays the piano daily, writes poetry, travels the country by train visiting relatives, and takes my bus when he's home to meet new people, go to new places and do new things. Eddy has taught me the secret to life and it is this: *The goal in life is to live young, have fun, and arrive at your final destination as late as possible, with a smile on your face.* It is such a powerful lesson and has made such a difference in my life I made it rule #10. Show him, Danny.

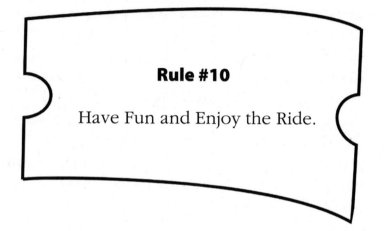

Rule #10

Have Fun and Enjoy the Ride.

"And you know what the final destination I'm talking about is, right, George? No one can escape it. We're all going there. But the important thing is how much we enjoy the ride until we get there. After all, we only have one life and one ride. This is not like Disney Land. We only get one ride so we might as well enjoy it to the max.

"Too many people think they are going to live forever. They spend their life accumulating wealth, possessions, and power only to leave it all when their bus ride is over. It's not like you can take it with you. So what's all the fuss about? Too many people stress over too many meaningless things. People get all protective of their turf. Just watch the news. Even countries argue over borders. If people only woke up they'd realize the whole universe is their home. Why fight over small pieces of territory when you can claim the universe as yours? Any moment they can have it all by simply enjoying the ride, but instead people focus on the small instead of living large. They worry about promotions, deadlines, e-mails, and argue with co-workers and family members about the minutest things forgetting that they will never see today again.

"Their bus is going through life but they are blind to the beauty around them. Think about it. The day you die you will still have 30 or 40 e-mails in your in-box that will not be answered. You'll never get it all done so you might as well relax, take a deep breath, and enjoy the ride. Tell him about that study of ninety-five-year-olds, Marty."

Marty perked up. "I love this study. They asked a bunch of ninety-five-year-olds, I don't know where they found them all, Florida I guess, but anyway they asked them if they could do it all over again and live their life again what would they do differently. The three things that almost all of them said were: (1) They would reflect more. Enjoy more moments. More sunrises and sunsets. More moments of joy. (2) They would take more risks and chances. Life is too short not to go for it. (3) They would have left a legacy. Something that would live on after they die.

"So you see what I'm saying, George. Learn from Eddy here. Learn from the ninety-five-year-olds. Don't go through life with regrets. Don't be someone who looks back and says I should have done this or that. Live and work like you have nothing to lose and everything to gain. Act like a kid on Christmas morning that is always optimistic and excited about the gifts you are receiving. Don't be too stressed to feel blessed. Don't compare the success of your bus to other buses. Just enjoy your ride. You go into that presentation today and you step on that gas pedal, have fun, and go for it. And when you blow them away and they sing your praises you just continue to live and work each day with purpose and joy. And that's easy to remember because all you got to do is remember me, the ultimate Joy." Then she looked up, laughed and said, "I know, God. Sometimes I can get a little too big for my britches."

Then as the energy bus approached George's office building she turned to George, who was quietly saving his voice for the presentation, and told him, "And when it comes to legacies remember this: The best legacy you could leave is not some building that is named after you or a piece of jewelry but rather a world that has been impacted and touched by your presence, your joy, and your positive actions."

The bus stopped and before George could get off the bus the passengers came forward to give him high fives, handshakes, and hugs. Jack handed George his business card and asked that George call him to let him know how the presentation had gone, since everyone on the bus would want to know. Of course Joy gave him the biggest

145

Game Day

hug of all and as George walked off the bus, she stood from the top of the stairs and said, "Today is your day, George. And this is your life. You came on my bus for a reason, like I told you. That reason is today and every day after."

George walked into the building thinking that this could be the last time he'd walk through these doors as an employee of the NRG Company or it could be his first day on the job as the Chief Energy Officer. In less than two hours he would know his fate, but regardless of the outcome he believed his bus was headed in the right direction and he was ready to enjoy the rest of his ride.

Chapter 32

The Presentation

 The top executives were sitting around the conference table expecting a disaster. They had high hopes for George early on but all they knew was that his performance was getting worse by the month and today would be his last day. Today would be the final straw. The NRG-2000 was to be officially launched by the company in a month and this presentation would determine if the product team was on track or in disarray as usual. They would in all likelihood place a senior executive to work with the product team and replace George. The NRG-2000 was their next big product push that would take their revenue to an all-time high, and they certainly couldn't place the future of their company in him.

George stood at the front of the room and looked into their eyes. He could see their negativity and doubt. He knew they were expecting him to crumble and fail. Why wouldn't they, he thought. His heart started to race and he found himself not able to think. Fear was starting to overtake him. Not now, he thought. I cannot allow them to bring me down.

He remembered Joy telling him that his positive energy must be greater than anyone's negativity, and in that one thought he found a smiling face staring at him. He thought of Joy, took a deep breath, and an incredible calm came over him. There certainly would be more failures in his life but not today. Today he would not be allowed to fail.

The executives were expecting a complete disaster but George and his team delivered one of the best product launches ever seen. His bus was cruising and the executives all jumped on for the ride.

After the presentation George and his team gave each other a group hug and the executives all flocked to George with pleasantly surprised looks of shock on their faces wanting to know how he had just done so great. "I decided it was time that I stopped being just a manager and started being a Chief Energy Officer," he told them. They had no idea what he was talking about but it didn't matter. George wasn't going anywhere except to meet with his team. He would have plenty of time to explain to the execs how to get on their energy bus and develop Chief Energy Officers. But for today he would take it easy, give his team the day off, and let them know how much he appreciated all they had done. Today they hit a home run in the bottom of the ninth inning with the bases loaded and it was cause for celebration.

But interestingly enough when George told his team

they could all go home and enjoy the day off, none of them wanted to leave. They all wanted to celebrate with the team and George. They wanted to savor the sweet smell of victory and soak up the energy of the moment together. George began to understand that a team who puts their heart and soul into a project and works hard toward a shared purpose wants to celebrate together. They had accomplished something amazing and they deserved to bask in the light of a job well done. He couldn't deny them that. They were his team and he loved them now more than ever. So instead of sending them home George invited them all to lunch where he treated them to an afternoon of food, fun, and unofficial team building. The team talked about their success today and their plans of continued success for the road ahead. They knew where their bus was going and they were excited about being on it.

Chapter 33

Joy

 The repair shop was just about to close when in the nick of time George walked in to pick up his car. He was thinking about the incredible lunch he had just had with his team when he approached the counter and said hello to the young lady who stood on the other side. She had red hair, a sweet expression, and a name tag that made George laugh. Her name was Joy. "What's so funny?" she asked.

"Nothing," he answered. "I just love your name. That's all." Then he looked up toward the ceiling and said, Thank you. The signs were clear. He realized that less than two weeks ago he had been cursing the heavens for bringing all the misfortune and misery into his life and now they were on his side guiding him and showing him the path every step of the way. He understood how everything, including the good and bad had brought him to this moment. If he had never gotten a flat tire he would never have met Joy. If he hadn't gone through all the adversity and challenges at work he would never have wanted to learn how to better lead his team.

Now his career and future were brighter than he could have ever imagined. If his wife hadn't threatened to leave him he never would have realized how bad things were and how good they could be. What he had thought was bad, he now realized led to good. Joy had told him that everything happens for a reason, and while he couldn't see it while he had been going through it, now everything was crystal clear.

Life is a test. Every adversity helps us grow. Negative events and people teach us what we don't want so we can focus our energy on what we do want. George made a mental note that the next time he faced a problem at work, because he knew there would always be new challenges, he would not let the problem sweep him up and swirl him around like a tornado. Rather from now on he would ask, What can I learn from this challenge? What is it teaching me? Then he would stay positive and trust that the lessons would make him stronger, wiser, and better.

The woman behind the counter gave him his keys and said, "Enjoy your car, Sir. I bet you are glad to have it back."

George thanked her as he walked outside toward his car with the word "enjoy" lingering in his mind. He thought it was amazing how joy kept coming up in his life and how it flowed through him right now and spoke to his heart. It told him not to focus too much on the places he has been but only to learn from the past. It said, Do not focus on the future because the future brings only what the present gives it. Rather, his heart whispered, Focus on the path. Keep your head up and your heart full of joy. George realized that for all the lessons he had learned the past two weeks the greatest lesson of all had been right in front of him. It hadn't been something that must be said but something that had been experienced and felt. He knew that no matter where his energy bus took him and whatever roadblocks lay ahead, all he had to remember was to allow joy to flow through him and savor every moment and mile on his journey. If he filled his life with joy, his work with joy, and his home with joy, oh what a life he would live and oh what a ride it would be. With joy everything would flow better and easier.

As George drove his newly repaired car home, he made a commitment to himself to experience the joy in everything he did. Whether he was working on a project at work or spending time with his kids at home he told himself that he would ask, Where's the joy in this moment? Do I feel it? How can I experience more joy right now? He had experienced what it was like to ride on Joy's bus and now he would make the feeling of joy a permanent passenger on his bus.

George reached for his cell phone and called his mother. She had just finished her latest bout with chemo and George knew she could use some joy right now. He wanted to tell her to enjoy every moment she had left whether it was six months or six years. He wanted to tell her to savor the joy of every second and fill up with love not fear during this challenging time and every day of her life thereafter. He hoped somehow his own joy could relieve her of her anger and pain. But when she picked up the phone George knew he didn't need to say any of those things. It wasn't something he could teach with words. It was something she needed to experience. He knew all he needed to say was, "I love you" from the depths of his heart.

Chapter 34

It's More Fun on the Bus

 When Bus #11 pulled up to the bus stop on Monday, George jumped on. He gave Joy a big hug and then shouted to the rest of the bus, "We did it! The presentation went perfect!" The passengers cheered wildly as George high-fived Jack, Danny, Marty, and the rest of the passengers. Then he reached down next to his briefcase and lifted up a big sign.

"What's that, Sugar?" asked Joy.

"It's a new sign," answered George. "If people will learn the 10 rules, they should be able to read the rules on your bus. You can't read the handwritten words on your current sign up there so I wanted to give you something bold and clear that will allow you to help others in the same way you helped me."

"You are too sweet, George. And look at how pretty it is with those nice white bold letters. The rules look real good."

"Let's put it up," Marty said from the back of the bus and the rest of the passengers agreed.

So they put up George's sign, which would proudly

proclaim the Energy Bus rules for all future passengers and drivers to see.

They were the 10 rules that had changed George's life, and everyone else on the bus knew this was only the beginning. Joy knew there would be many more Georges and Janes to come on her bus, and she was ready for all of them.

"Well, George, I want you to know that everyone who comes on the bus from now on will know your story," Joy said as she pointed to the sign. "While you are driving that fancy car of yours to work your ears will be ringing because we will tell them about the man who gave us this sign and how he courageously plowed through the darkness to find his light. We will tell your success story, George."

"Well, that's nice and all," George said, "and I'm truly honored but if you are going to talk about me, it will have to be in front of me. Because I guess you can say I've had a change of heart. I've decided to take the bus to work from now on. Driving your car to work is great but it's more fun on the bus!!"

"Yes, it is. It certainly is more fun on the bus," Joy said giving him a big bright smile. George smiled back as she stepped on the gas pedal and took off to the next bus stop where someone, somewhere was waiting for the Energy Bus. They would get on and it wouldn't take long for them to learn what George now knew.

The Energy Bus will surely take you on the ride of your life.

10 RULES FOR THE RIDE OF YOUR LIFE

1. You're the driver of the your bus.

2. Desire, vision, and focus move your bus in the right direction.

3. Fuel your ride with positive energy.

4. Invite people on your bus and share your vision for the road ahead.

5. Don't waste your energy on those who don't get on your bus.

6. Post a sign that says NO ENERGY VAMPIRES ALLOWED on your bus.

7. Enthusiasm attracts more passengers and energizes them during the ride.

8. Love your passengers.

9. Drive with purpose.

10. Have fun and enjoy the ride.

The Energy Bus Action Plan

 Utilize the Energy Bus principles to build a positive, high performing team.

A simple, powerful practice for businesses, organizations, schools, churches, sports teams, and even families.

Step 1: Create Your Vision

Gather your team and spend time developing a vision for where you want your bus to go. You may present a vision to them and ask for input or you may start with a blank slate and develop the vision together. You might create one vision or several visions.

Questions to ask

- What are our goals?
- Think into the future. What do we see?
- What do we hope to accomplish?

Step 2: Fuel Your Vision with Purpose

As you create your vision you'll want to associate it with a larger and bigger purpose.

> *Questions you may want to ask to develop your purpose*
>
> - How will our vision benefit the growth of the individuals who make up the team?
> - How will our vision benefit others?
> - What greatness can we strive for?
> - What do we stand for?
> - How can we make a difference?

Step 3: Write Down Your Vision/Purpose Statement

Incorporate your vision and purpose into one powerful vision statement and write it down.

Step 4: Focus on Your Vision

- Make a copy of your Vision/Purpose Statement and hand it out to your team.

- Encourage each team member to review the vision daily.
- Ask each team member to visualize the team achieving their vision for 10 minutes a day.

Step 5: Zoom Focus

- Identify the goals your team needs to achieve to make your vision a reality.
- Write these goals down.
- Identify the action steps necessary to achieve the goals that will make your vision a reality.
- Write down these action steps.
- Make a copy of these goals and action steps and give to each team member.

Step 6: Get on the Bus

- Identify who else needs to be on the bus to help you implement the action steps that will achieve the goals and vision you and your team have set.
- Invite them on the bus. Visit www.theenergybus.com and e-mail them an e-bus ticket or hand deliver a printed ticket.

Step 7: Fuel the Ride with Positive Energy and Enthusiasm

- Engage and energize your employees on a daily basis filling the void with positive energy so negativity can't breed.

- Incorporate practices and processes that cultivate a culture of positive energy.

- Visit www.jongordon.com for proven solutions and best practices.

Step 8: Post a Sign that Says "No Energy Vampires Allowed"

- Identify the negative team members who are affecting the success of your bus ride.

- Open the lines of communication. Let them know they are being negative. Determine if there is a justifiable reason. Determine a course of action that will lead to individual and team success. Encourage them to get on the bus with positive energy. Give them a chance to succeed.

- If they fail to make changes and continue to be negative, then you have no choice but to let them off the bus.

Step 9: **Navigate Adversity and Potholes**

Expect that every great team, including yours, will face adversity, challenges, and struggles along the ride. Every great team will be tested, but great teams don't let flat tires stop them from reaching their destination.

> *When faced with a challenge, setback, or adversity ask the following questions.*
>
> - What can we learn from this challenge?
> - What is this problem teaching us?
> - How can we grow from this adversity?
> - What opportunity does this challenge present to our team?

Build upon your challenges and use them to pave the road to success.

Step 10: **Love Your Passengers**

During the course of your ride, as you drive toward your vision and purpose, let your fellow drivers and passengers know you care about them.

> *Ask the following questions*
>
> - How can I recognize them?
> - How can I spend valuable time with them?

- How can I better listen to them?
- How can I serve them and their growth?
- How can I bring out the best in them? How can I energize their strengths to better themselves and the team?

Visit www.jongordon.com for practices to bring out the best in your people and team.

Step 11: Have Fun and Enjoy the Ride

- Remember that every bus trip and journey should be fun.
- It doesn't have to be a difficult and painful ride.
- Ask your team regularly how we can be more successful and have more fun in the process.
- Ask how we can bring more joy to the work we do.
- Remind yourself and your team that the goal of every journey should be to arrive at your destination with a smile on your face. It's not just about the destination but about the team you become along the way.

Remember, you have only one ride through life so give it all you got and enjoy the ride.

Visit **www.TheEnergyBus.com** to:

- Send bus tickets via e-mail to your company, organization, school, team, family, and friends and invite them to share the energy
- Print customized bus tickets to mail or hand deliver
- Launch, announce, and garner support for a new initiative
- Enhance individual and group morale, productivity, and performance

If you are interested in leadership, sales, customer service and team-building programs based on *The Energy Bus* principles, **contact The Jon Gordon Companies** at:

830-13 A1A N.
Suite 111
Ponte Vedra Beach, FL32082
info@jongordon.com
(904) 285-6842

Sign up for Jon's weekly newsletter at JonGordon.com. Follow him on Twitter at @JonGordon11.

THE
ENERGY BUS
TRAINING PROGRAM

A TRAINING TOOL TO FUEL YOUR LIFE, WORK, AND TEAM WITH POSITIVE ENERGY

The Energy Bus Training Program is an innovative online training platform to help you and your team harness the power of positive energy.

- A 60-minute course featuring an **animated video** retelling of The Energy Bus story, and video commentary by Jon Gordon himself
- Interactive exercises tied to each module
- A customized action plan to help you implement Jon Gordon's 10 Rules and fuel your life, work, and team with positive energy
- Lessons to enhance your positivity and performance
- Management tools to organize and track the progress of your team

Powerful. Scalable. Enjoyable. **The Energy Bus Training Program** is an energizing vehicle for transporting your organization to new heights of accomplishment.

Get on board The Energy Bus

Learn how this innovative new training program can energize the lives of you and your team.

✓ Brings The Best-Selling Book to Life.

✓ Transforms Everyday Adversity Into Positive Results.

✓ Brings Out the Best In Your Self and Your Teams.

✓ Turns Negativity Into Positive Engagement.

Get on The Bus today!

You and your team will be glad you did.

Learn more at **energybustraining.com**

Wiley is a registered trademark of John Wiley & Sons, Inc.

Other Books by Jon Gordon

No Complaining Rule

Follow a VP of Human Resources who must save herself and her company from ruin, and discover proven principles and an actionable plan to win the battle against individual and organizational negativity.

www.NoComplainingRule.com

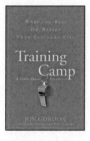

Training Camp

This inspirational story about a small guy with a big heart and a special coach who guides him on a quest for excellence reveals the eleven winning habits that separate the best individuals and teams from the rest.

www.TrainingCamp11.com

The Shark and the Goldfish

Delightfully illustrated, this quick read is packed with tips and strategies on how to respond to challenges beyond your control in order to thrive during the waves of change.

www.SharkandGoldfish.com

Soup

The newly anointed CEO of a popular soup company is brought in to reinvigorate the brand and bring success back to a company that has fallen on hard times. Through her journey, discover the key ingredients to unite, engage, and inspire teams and create a culture of greatness.

www.Soup11.com

The Seed

Go on a quest for the meaning and passion behind work with Josh, an up-and-comer at his company who is disenchanted with his job. Through Josh's cross-country journey, you'll find surprising new sources of wisdom and inspiration in your own business and life.

www.Seed11.com

The Energy Bus for Kids

This illustrated children's adaptation of the bestselling *The Energy Bus* tells the story of George who, with the help of his school bus driver Joy, learns that if he believes in himself, he'll find the strength to overcome any challenge. His journey teaches kids how to overcome negativity, bullies, and everyday challenges to be their best.

www.EnergyBusKids.com

Index

171

Index